To R.J.
In appr—
your work!

Of Spirits:
The Book Of Rowan

By Ivo Domínguez, Jr.
Panpipe

SapFire
www.sapfire.com

Of Spirits: The Book Of Rowan

Published by

SapFire Productions, Inc.
14914 Deer Forest Road
Georgetown, DE 19947, USA
(302) 855-0699 • orders@sapfire.com • www.sapfire.com

Copyright © 2001 By Ivo Dominguez, Jr. - *Panpipe*

All rights reserved. No part of this book may be reproduced or transmitted in any form or by any means, electronic or mechanical, including photocopying, recording or by any informational storage or retrieval system without permission in writing from the publisher except for brief quotes used in reviews or scholarly work.

Illustrations and layout by Ivo Dominguez, Jr. - *Panpipe*

Of Spirits is the second book in the Wheel of Trees series

Note: You are responsible for your actions. Neither the author nor the publisher are liable for your use of the information and methods presented in this book .

ISBN 0-9654198-1-9

SapFire

Printed and Bound in the United States

By Ivo Dominguez, Jr. - *Panpipe*

Table Of Contents

I.	A Journey Of No Steps	1
II.	Preparations And Interventions For Higher Order Workings	9
III.	Mediumship, Channeling, & Mediation	35
IV.	Impediments To Clear Spirit Contact	47
V.	Ghosts & Ancestors	57
VI.	Divine Embodiment	79
VII.	Spiritual Lineage, Egregores, & Sponsors	107
VIII.	The Great Ones	123
IX.	Closing Thoughts	135

Appendices 137

Acknowledgements & Dedications

This book is dedicated to James C. Welch and Adam J. Murta whose love, support, and encouragement made this work possible. I would also like to recognize all my companions in The Assembly Of The Sacred Wheel. Their steadfast openness, energy, and kindness is without peer. I would also like to acknowledge the influence of three special women whose example put me to the task of this book.

Dearest Ahkleviah, Lyrata, and Shevierah, thank you!

A Journey Of No Steps

It is easier to write when you have an audience in mind so this book was written for intermediate level practitioners. Unfortunately there is no standard set of benchmarks for what constitutes an intermediate knowledge of the sacred sciences. Additionally, traditions vary in the order in which they teach their material and all systems have gaps in their knowledge. So *intermediate* for the purpose of this book, means enough education and actual experience in esoteric matters so that it is possible to make educated guesses and to connect new information to your existing knowledge base in a orderly fashion. If you are a novice you can gain benefit from this book if you are willing to take extra time with each chapter and to research the words and concepts that are new to you.

I begin this book with self-disclosure because all matters related to working with the spirits is intensely personal and for you to make the best use of what I have to say requires some insight into my inner life. In preparing to write this book I asked for the help of the spirit of the Rowan tree as the voice of the Rowan has the power to call the spirits. I honor the assistance I did receive through invoking that name. Having opened myself to guidance and vowing to listen to it, I discovered that what you ask for is often granted though sometimes the gift itself is a challenge. I had all but finished this book when I was given the very strong and clear message that the work was a good preparation and that I was ready to begin. I was confident that what I had written was solid material, but over the course of several weeks in dialogues with several beings I became convinced that it was time to begin again. With some heart wrenching and hand wringing, I deleted the many chapters and the outline I had written from my computer. I did this with confidence that comes from an *informed subjectivity* that I believe is necessary for safe and sane work with the unseen. So this book comes to you delayed by over a year but mellowed and deepened by the sacrifice of starting over again. The effort that went into that first draft, that now only exists in the other realms, has greatly enriched the classes that I give. Phrases, similes, and insights from that work now add flavor and focus to many other endeavors.

Of Spirits: The Book Of Rowan

Contact with nonphysical beings has been a part of my life since I was a child and I have fairly clear memories back to about age three. I became aware of a difference between my invisible friends and those that the other children in my neighborhood had when I was six. Like many children, I had invisible friends that were like toys, imaginary constructs with whom I could play and whose actions I could control. I also had invisible friends that had a life of their own, and the discovery that not everyone had such friends was a revelation. Whether it was by grace, fate, guidance, or past life memories I neither know nor care to know, but I have, since that early age, treated nonphysical beings much as I would those of flesh. As a child, this meant that if I was deceived or treated poorly by them, they would cease to be my friends. As I grew older and my understanding of life expanded, I applied the essence of what I learned in the mundane world to the other realms. It seemed to me that the general rules of civil behavior and safety should apply on more than one Plane of Being.

This perspective and its associated attitudes have served me well and safeguarded me from more than one situation. It is only in the last few years that I have come to appreciate just how fortunate I am in this regard.

A Note On Terms

As a general rule I will be using the word "spirit" as an all inclusive term

---

🌳 Rowan's Voice Calls The Spirits 🌳

European Mountain Ash, *Sorbus aucuparia*
Other Names: Delight of the Eye, Quicken, Witchwood, Sorb Apple, Royne Tree

Rowan is a tree that is sacred in many parts of Europe and especially so in the British Isles. It was brought to the Americas where it has established itself as a wild tree. One of the myths of the Rowan is that it was originally from the realm of Faerie and was brought to Earth by the Tuatha De Danaan. Rowan has extensive connections with the realm of Faerie. Groves of Rowans are associated with oracular sites such as on the Amber Islands of the Baltic. Single or small clumps of Rowan are associated with stone circles throughout all of Western Europe.

There is disagreement among practitioners whether the energy of the Rowan more closely resonates to that of the Moon, the Sun, or Uranus, but there is general agreement that its element is fire. I suspect that all three planetary assignments apply because it is a tree of thresholds and all liminal states. Moreover, its true element is probably light of which fire is one manifestation. Rowan has the power to open and to close gates, to summon and to banish, to protect and to sustain. All parts of the tree are useful for the making of incense or magickal tools.

The berries were used by the Druids and Welsh witches in brewing wines and potions that increased the power of the second sight. The blossom end of the berry is marked with a natural pentacle. If the berries are charged in a ritual they achieve special vital energy potency so that if one berry is consumed it gives the prana of nine meals. Very useful for healing, strenuous work, and fasting. Even without the ritual, 1 berry quartered and brewed as a tea greatly increases second sight.

for all beings who do not have a physical body. This usage will encompass the full range of beings from discarnate humans to Deities. I will also use the phrase "Great One" to refer to beings that are very far above our stage of development. Depending upon your beliefs and faith community the Great Ones may include beings that are Archons, Arch-Angels, Demi-God/dess/es, Lords of Karma, God/dess/es, and so on. I will also often change my word choice in referring to the same phenomena such as Planes of Being, Planes of Reality, Levels, etc. I do this in deference to the diversity of the readers and also as a reminder that all these terms represent only a small portion of what they label. As you read, mentally adjust the terms to match those that you use and be mindful of any additional information that comes from the comparison of the expressions.

Informed Subjectivity

Objectivity is an impossibility in matters related to spirit contact. Some might argue that objectivity is impossible in all human endeavors, but there can be no question that communication with beings through the instrument of our consciousness is always influenced by all those distinctions that make us individuals. A certain amount of error, distortion, and misinterpretation is a part of all spirit contact and if it is maintained at a low level, it does little harm. A greater hazard comes from the desires, fears, and expectations that we bring to this work. The first step then in improving the quality of spirit contact is an exploration of our own biases and predispositons. So while objectivity may be unattainable, it is possible to develop a working approximation of objectivity that I call *informed subjectivity*. This type of self-awareness consists of many things, but there are a few factors that have a greater impact in developing an informed subjectivity than others.

It is essential to become aware of those things that are triggers that cause emotional responses. We cannot, nor should we try, to eliminate our emotional nature. The repression of the emotions only moves the emotions to a place in our being where we have less conscious control. Moreover, repressed emotions build in pressure and are often released in unexpected ways. The emotions, which are often correlated to the Element of Water, are reflective, reactive, and absorptive. Emotions are also like water in that they take on the shape of their container and are more likely to remain wholesome if they are flowing. By becoming aware of our emotional nature we can work with our emotions by becoming proper vessels and proper conduits for each situation. Becoming aware of the situations or the concepts that provoke strong emotional responses is not the same as the desensitization methods used in controlling fears, the reverse is what is needed. It is only by fully experiencing our emotions that we can develop the insight needed to hold ourselves in a good relationship to them.

These recommendations to plumb the depths of your emotions pertain as much to the reader that thinks of themselves as volatile as to the reader that thinks of themselves as stolid. In fact, the most insidious effects that mar clarity are those that are less dramatic. Gentle or low key emotional responses walk meekly past defenses that are set to stop their more dramatic kin. Deep communication is full of details and nuances that can be subtly altered by these emotions that are camouflaged by the appearance of acceptability.

Spiritual entities often have information, attitudes, and perspectives that are quite different or distant from human sentiment and cognition. When we translate from one human language to another, often it is difficult to convey exactly the same message because of cultural differences. Even within our own cultures, when we read literature from a few centuries ago, we must often puzzle out the meaning. When it comes to the sciences, sacred or mundane, each discipline has its own specialized jargon or terms of art to convey their knowledge. More than once, I have heard friends tell me that listening to the conversations of astrologers is like listening to a foreign language. To strive for an informed subjectivity also means developing a wide breadth of knowledge in both the arts and the sciences. The more comprehensive the range of what has been perceived, discovered, or learned by an individual, the more likely it is that they will be able to grasp the import of spiritual communications. In my own experience, I have gleaned as many spiritual and magickal insights from what I learned in Geology and Physics classes as I have in coursework on Milton or Jung. The following is a statement by Sri Aurobindo that should be read and reread by all those that aspire to productive spirit contact.

> *"It is necessary, therefore, that advancing knowledge should base herself on a clear, pure and disciplined intellect. It is necessary, too, that she should correct her errors, sometimes by a return to the restraint of sensible fact, the concrete realities of the physical world. The touch of Earth is always reinvigorating to the sons of Earth ... the superphysical can only be really mastered in its fullness ... when we keep our feet firmly on the physical."*
>
> — Sri Aurobindo as quoted by W. T. Stace in *The Teachings Of The Mystics*.

This statement also leads us to perhaps the most important part of an informed subjectivity and that is the value of corroboration and supporting evidence in spirit contact. The spirits and any communications purported to be from spirits must be tested. Just as trust, respect, and admiration build up over time with the people in your life, the same is true for the spirits. If you were to seek out professional counsel for a business matter, it would be prudent to check their references and their past performance. Any information or advice that has significant consequences should be examined carefully before it is accepted and especially before it is put into action. Sometimes people are reluctant to test the spirits. It may be that they do not want to offend or that they consider it arrogant to question beings of light. The spirits are not all exalted beings, some are pranksters, some are scoundrels, some are paragons of virtue, and others can be everything in between. An intelligent and enlightened being will be understanding of the intent behind our efforts to verify information or to determine the nature of the spirit. Conversely, your understanding of their efforts is needed. Spiritual entities are not infallible, with the exception of beings with whom we rarely have contact. The information they offer with good intention can end up being wrong or misused. It is important for you to have reasonable expectations about the value and accuracy of information gained through spirit contact. So long as free will exists, the future is always in flux.

In addition to testing the spirits, we must test ourselves. The supposed objectivity of science is based to a great degree upon the repeatability of observations. Something analogous is possible in spiritual matters, but the rules of evidence must be modified. Whenever possible check your psychic perceptions against those of another person's psychic perceptions. While it is certainly true that even if two people are perceiving the same spirit at the same time it is likely that they will have different descriptions, there should be symbolic and thematic correspondences between their experiences. If there are not sufficient correspondences, then the source of the communication or the reality of the contact should be in question. I cannot offer an easy guideline to make this determination, only experience and discernment can tell what is sufficient. With repeated verifications and contradictions of your perceptions you can come closer to having an informed subjectivity in regards to your psychic capacities. It goes almost without saying that an incisive and honest self-assessment of your wishes and fears is a prerequisite to understanding how we color the information we do receive.

The Elements Of Being

Contact and communication with the spirits is a touching of *being* to *being* when it occurs at the highest Planes of Reality. Most spirit contact occurs at much lower levels and is better thought of as a touching of *consciousness* to *consciousness*. Regardless of the level of the contact, that communication can be thought of as having three primary components: *energy, information,* and *essence*. The higher you rise on the Planes, the less distinction there is between these components, and indeed at the highest level they coalesce into pure being. As you descend closer to the Earth Plane, energy, information, and essence gradually separate and become manifestly discrete. As you descend there are also differences in the relative ease of perception and connection that humans experience. Energy is the easiest to sense on the lower planes and Essence is the easiest to sense on the higher planes. Information is experienced as strongest in the middle planes and less so above and below.

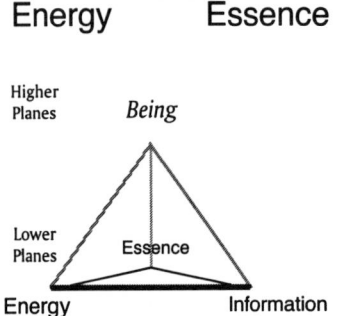

Essence, Information, & Energy

Essence can be compared to the chromosomes in a fertilized egg or a seed in that it is the map for the possibilities of development and unfolding. It is also like a mathematical formula that of itself is a small thing but produces a complicated three dimensional graph when numbers are plugged into it. Essence is the go-between, the intermediary between the unmanifest and the manifest, the implicate and the explicate. This is the domain of the mystic. Essence is the way of knowing and being expressed by fractals and chaos theory. Essence is more closely associated with the Higher Self and the Neschamah.

Information is a description of relationships between things. It is an orderly collection of facts or data. Information can be a sequence of interrelated actions. This is the realm of thought. It can be summarizing statements like the laws of physics. If *information* can be compared to the laws of physics, then *essence* is the invisible agency that produces the phenomena that those laws describe. Information is the way of knowing and being expressed by the microcosm-macrocosm paradigm and the scale model. Information is more closely associated with the Middle Self and the Ruach.

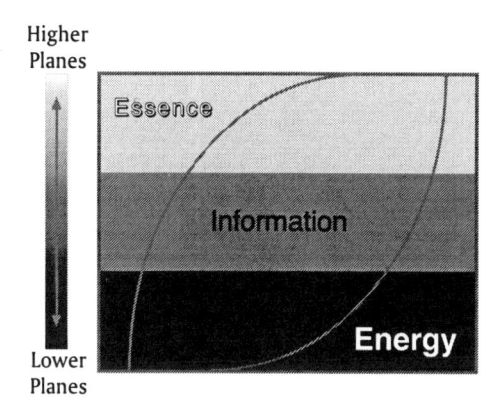

Energy conveys itself. It expresses its contents through interaction. Energy is neither the pattern for a process nor is it a conceptualization of the pattern. A beam of red light is red, and when we see it we do so by absorbing some of it. Energy affects us by creating sensation and experience. Emotion and passion are strongly energetic. Energy, used in this sense, is the carrier wave for manifestation. Energy is the way of knowing and being expressed by the interwoven wavefronts of a hologram and a gestalt. Energy is more closely associated with the Lower Self and the Nephesch.

A Journey Of No Steps

The process of developing depth and proficiency in spirit work can be compared to the same process in the art and science of music. Anyone who can hear music can be moved, can be swept away, by the tides of emotion that the masterpieces of music can stir. In just such a manner, anyone who is receptive can sense the more powerful flows of energy, information, and essence involved in spirit communication. For many people, listening to music with an uneducated, but appreciative ear is enough. For some, sensing the presence and the contact of discarnate beings with an untutored soul is also enough. Those that wish to understand more must learn more. Those that would perform, compose, and collaborate must be willing to commit to both study and practice. It is true in both spirit contact and music that if you do not have the ear for it, no amount of study will suffice.

There is a Chinese proverb that says that the longest journey begins with a single step. The work and the time required to become skilled at spirit contact is lengthy. Perhaps the first step is in making peace with that requirement and in overcoming inertia so that the first step is followed by many more. These are internal steps, and it may be better to say that this is a journey of no steps. This is a journey of self exploration, of the integration of the dense physical self with the subtle ethereal selves, and of the integration of the many levels of consciousness that make up our being. Therefore, this is a journey that for the most part must be undertaken alone, but it is valuable to compare notes with fellow travelers. In fact, it is my experience that very few are successful without the help of companions. This book summarizes some of my impressions from the travel log of my journey. My hope is that reading these impressions will aid you in planning a safer and more direct route for your journey of no steps.

Preparations And Interventions For Higher Order Workings

This chapter belongs both near the beginning and at the end of this book. On the one hand, it presents information that is helpful to understanding subsequent chapters and as such belongs near the beginning. On the other hand, much of the material in this chapter is better understood after reading the remainder of this book. I have placed it here near the beginning, but I hope that you will return to it later. If you intend to put into practice the techniques and interventions described here, it is my hope that you will read this chapter several times.

Overview

As the level of magickal expertise rises, there will also be an increase in the energy level and the intensity of rituals. Some may argue that the level of magickal expertise is dropping instead of rising. Both statements are true in reference to the observations that they describe. What is more generally true is that we are in a time wherein the number of people engaged in rituals, ceremonies, and magickal workings is growing. This increase in numbers results in more rituals, covering the full spectrum of efficacy, and that increase in energy output has its impact on the other realms. If an overgrown path through the woods has an increase in traffic, it will quickly become clear of debris and the passage of many feet will smooth and mark the way. The same is true for the ways between worlds so that travel to the other realms becomes easier even for those who are neither guides nor trackers. Incarnate humans are becoming more and more visible on the other planes. When we are in rituals or are engaged in other activities that transfer more of our focus of consciousness to the other planes, we are more present and palpable to the beings that are resident there. All these factors combined increase the likelihood for greater participation on the part of spirits in our magick. Greater presence of spiritual beings in our rituals means that in addition to the proper management of energy that most ritualists focus on, there is a need to manage the interactions between different kinds and orders of consciousness.

Moreover, during the change of the Ages that we live in, the attributes of the veils between the planes of being are in flux. The change of the Age can also be thought of as a location where the weather changes swiftly and with little warning. We may find ourselves in rituals or workings where we prepared ourselves for a particular set of influences only to find them changing during our efforts. This instability also resembles the changing of a tide in that although the overall direction of the flow is clear, there are chaotic swirls, eddies, and quiet points as the tide churns and sweeps through its environment. The watery tides of the physical world are fairly constant with some adjustments for the Moon's position, the weather, and the landscape. The energetic tides accompanying the movement from the Age of Pisces to the Age of Aquarius are much more complex. The turning of the Ages is magnitudes of order larger than the turning of the tides, and the increase in scale of the phenomena increases the complexity and the chaotic elements of the change. Additionally, the energetic tide is operating on all the planes of being below the Abyss, and each of these operates within its own type and rate of time.

This combination of ingredients will probably result in an increase in the frequency and severity of powerful, sometimes adverse, reactions to ritual. This is not necessarily a bad thing, because often these crises are gateways to development and to spiritual evolution, but only if they are provided a proper conditions and context. While it may be true that those things that do not kill us only make us stronger, an untended wound can result in restrictive scar tissue. Injuries can also be avoided by preparation, and indeed many of the mishaps in rituals are a result of improper conditioning. Athletes know the value of stretching and warming up before strenuous activity. They also know that it is pointless or dangerous to attempt a vault to a height that far exceeds their level of preparation.

This chapter offers advice on choosing techniques to improve conditioning in order to cut down on injuries and a frame of reference for assessment and intervention in cases of unbalanced or abreactive responses to ritual and ceremony. It provides useful pointers and techniques, but does not pretend to be comprehensive. This is not a substitute for training. It is written with the assumption that the reader has at least an intermediate level of magickal proficiency. If that is not the case, the material is still useful for personal development, but don't overestimate what you can do for others. Additionally, the perspectives and ideas offered here will facilitate a deeper understanding of the knowledge gained in future studies.

Preparations And Interventions For Higher Order Workings

The information in this chapter is based partly on personal experience, partly on anecdotal information, and partly on spiritual guidance. I ask that you record your experiences in using the material from this chapter so that over time an element of science can refine our responses to these very special healing crises. A repertoire of specialized healing techniques and protocols will hopefully develop to provide the proper equilibrating force to the rising tide of change in the transitional period we live in.

Preparations

Strong And Balanced Development Of The Subtle Bodies

Magick is hard work, and the brunt of that work is borne by our energetic bodies. The first step in preventing injuries or adverse reactions from rituals or spirit contact is to improve the overall fitness of our subtle bodies. I have met people who felt that they were in good shape energetically only to find that their assessment of their fitness was mistaken when put to a hard test. The absence of illness is the beginning of fitness— not its end. Imagine two planks of wood, both of them free of warps, knots, and straight of grain. On the surface they appear similar but one is made of oak and the other of balsa wood. If they are to be placed as support beams in load bearing walls, the balsa will fail. A brightly colored aura with free flowing energy and no evidence of blockages is not proof of fitness.

In the physical body, the concept of fitness can be summarized as strength, flexibility, and cardiovascular capacity. In the subtle bodies, strength, flexibility, and capacity for flow also serve as starting points for describing fitness though the words have extended meanings.

• **Strength** is the capacity to direct one's energies to push or to pull with or against another flow of energy. Strength is also the ability to hold the shape of the subtle bodies constant against internal or external changes to energetic pressures or flows.

• **Flexibility** is demonstrated by the power to extend, to stretch, and to reshape the subtle bodies. The quality of flexibility is also expressed by the range and the distance of motion before there is a discontinuity, a crack, in the auric layers or a shearing or sliding that dislocates the alignments between subtle bodies.

- **Flow** is partly a measure of the volume and the rate of energy that can pass through or be controlled by the subtle bodies, but there is a more critical measure relative to preventing injury. The quality of the flow is greatly affected by the amount of constriction, resistance offered to the flow and the amount of turbulence introduced into the flow by irregularities in the subtle bodies.

By adding these parameters for subtle fitness to your awareness, it becomes possible to extend your psychic perceptions to better gauge readiness for trying workings. Psychic perceptions are also improved by including and applying what is known of the physical to the subtle. The words anatomy and physiology imply structures, complexity, and often a lengthy learning process to gain a working knowledge. Most people are aware of the marvels of form and function present in the physical body, and yet often people tend to think of the aura and subtle bodies as being simpler than the pattern of the body. This incongruity may in part be a result of the relatively low level of resolution that is common in the perception of the aura or perhaps it is an expression of the desire for the spiritual realms to be easier than those of matter. It is true that as you get further away from the physical plane of reality that there is greater plasticity in form and function but there is a balancing increase in other limitations to which the finer substance and energy must adhere. In all questions of matter, energy, and magick the equations of conservation, change, and exchange seek balance.

There are many methods for building strength, flexibility, and flow in the subtle bodies, and covering them exceeds the scope of this book. I encourage you to pursue this sort of fitness as vigorously as you would pursue physical fitness, academic training, and all the other avenues of development open to you. What I can offer are some perspectives on what constitutes a balanced program of development, and a technique that helps to integrate strength, flexibility, and flow. There are three broadly defined structural and functional sets within the subtle bodies that form a sensible approach to energetic fitness and they are: the chakras, the parts of self as described by the Elements and the Planes of Being, and the Central Column of energy.

The Chakras

The word chakra comes from the Sanskrit word for wheel, and indeed they do resemble spinning wheels or vortices of light. Often a chakra may be seen to pulse or spin in more than one direction at once which may

Preparations And Interventions For Higher Order Workings

seem improbable or disconcerting at first. The chakras are in constant motion and their forms change continually in response to inner changes and to the environment. In perceiving them, this motion and flux may or may not be apparent in the same manner that a spinning propeller may seem to be a disk or a whirling blade. Bear in mind that when you are dealing with subtle energies you are also dealing with subtle matter. This means that the limits for motion to which you have been accustomed may not hold true. Consider what happens if you take two lit flashlights and cross their beams. There is some interaction, but for the most part the beams continue in their own directions.

There are numerous systems to describe the chakras and most of them work well so long as you commit to working with the system you choose. The system that I prefer uses eight major chakras in the human aura. The first seven are personal and fully a part of the individual's subtle bodies and the eighth which is transpersonal and marks the place where the individual blends with the field of the universe. Each of the chakras exists in each layer of the aura. The chakras are the equivalent in the subtle bodies of the glands and organs in the body. The eight chakras are not the only chakras, rather they are the most important ones in the same sense that some organs of the body are more critical than others. Wherever in the aura there is a specialization of function you will find a vortex of energy and pattern that is a chakra. Although some of these minor chakras do correspond to organs or glands in the body others only do so in a metaphorical way. An example of this is the chakras in the hands and feet. The hands have a vortex at each finger and in the palm and the feet at each toe and the center of the arch. Our minds focus strongly on our hands and feet as our means to move and act in the world and that which is strong in the mind is form and substance on other Planes of Being. In this case this focus results in the formation of minor chakras in our hands and feet which are used to move and act on other planes. As a general rule any part of the body which has heightened physical sensitivity is also a site for a minor chakra or a line that marks energy flows

Subtle energy moves in and out of each chakra as if they were inhaling and exhaling the energy. This *respiration* occurs as a relatively independent activity with each subtle body (layer of the aura). This means that each chakra's energy intake and output is in effect a distinct functioning unit within each subtle body at the same time that it may be considered one chakra. Ideally there is a harmonious flow of suitable amounts of energy through all the layers but it is common for different layers of a chakra to exhibit different levels of strength and health. Physical, psychological, or

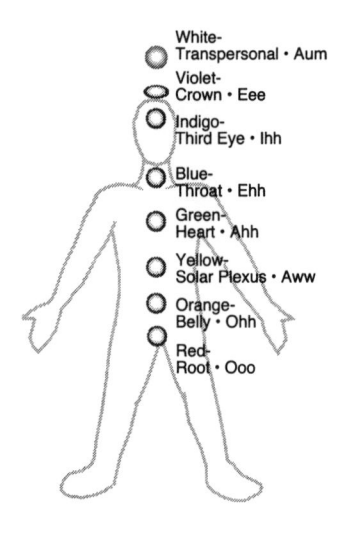

Figure labels (body diagram):
- White - Transpersonal · Aum
- Violet - Crown · Eee
- Indigo - Third Eye · Ihh
- Blue - Throat · Ehh
- Green - Heart · Ahh
- Yellow - Solar Plexus · Aww
- Orange - Belly · Ohh
- Red - Root · Ooo

spiritual problems often express themselves as improper flow and function on one or more layers in one or more chakras. Just as we carry stress and strain in our muscles and bones we also reflect these tensions in our subtle bodies. See figure on healthy and unhealthy states. Generally, so long as a person is living, each of the chakras must be somewhat functional and some amount of energy flow must be present within and between chakras. It may be hard to sense energies but that does not mean they do not exist. If a person is close to death or has a chronic degenerative illness some layers of the aura and some layers of chakras may indeed be virtually gone.

The flow and process in and out of a chakra relates to the health and strength of the functions housed in that chakra (see figures). The flow and

Chakra	Healthy States	Unhealthy States
Transpersonal	Identity With Higher Entities, Energy From The Whole, Evolution, Enlightenment, Higher Will	Loss Of Identity, Drained Of Vitality, Distortion Of Spirit, Soul's Growth Stunted
Crown	Creativity, Timeless, Wonder, Transformation, Divine Instinict, Bliss	Apathy, Jaded, Space Cadet, Negative Self-Image, Psychosis
Brow	Visionary, Psychism, Intuition, Trust In Life, Aesthetic Sense, Psi Gifts	Fear Of Future, Misguided, Unproductive, Stuck, Obsession
Throat	Conceptualization, Devotion, Synthesizing, Idealism, Creativity	Authoritarian, Rigid, Melancholy, Past Trapped, Repression
Heart	Nurturing, Safety, Vitality, Compassion, Unconditional Love, Joy	Stingy, Mistrust Of Life, Self-Doubting, Selfish, Bitterness
Solar Plexus	Analytical, Individuation, Self-Awareness, Understanding, Directive Will	Reductionist, Separate, Loss Of Feeling, Meaningless, Doubt, Guilt, Power Over Others
Belly	Altruism, Hospitable, Warm, Family/Group Consciousness, Well-being	Shallow, Power Hungry, Social Climbing, Deceit, Social Anxiety
Root	Spontaneous, Pragmatic, Now, Sexual, Manifesting, Real, Passion	Aggression, Obsession, Thoughtless, Rash, Bullying, Rage

process of energy from chakra to chakra relates to the strength and integration of the various functions and hence to a person's physical and psychological health. A person's emotional and psychological history and status is displayed more clearly in the chakras than in any other part of the subtle bodies. This information is only available if the focus of psychic perception shifts so as to see the chakra as it appears in each of the subtle bodies. Some people are able to learn to see all the overlain images at once, and others must learn to see one at a time and then puzzle the meaning together. Do not be distressed if you do not have the sight, there are other ways of sensing and knowing. The key point to remember is that you must strive to sense the chakra's various layers.

Although the chakras, the parts of self as described by the Elements and the Planes of Being, and the central column of energy each of have a role in determining energetic fitness, the chakras are the primary source of *strength*. The chakras may be strengthened and rebalanced up to a point by various exercises or by the intervention of a healer or energy worker. If the psychological or physical problems or situations that are inextricably linked to the chakras are not addressed directly, no amount of chakra work will help.

The Elements & The Three Selves

The use of the Four Elements plus Spirit or Ether to describe the building blocks that form the Self is a common practice in most of the magick of the West. The attributions of which qualities and characteristics belong to each element vary somewhat from system to system but in essence are consistent. As an example of the types of correlations made to the Elements, I have included the ones we use in the Assembly of the Sacred Wheel in this

Air	Fire	Water	Earth
The Mind-Thought	The Soul-Passion	The Heart-Emotions	The Body-Instinct
The East	The South	The West	The North
Dawn	Noon	Dusk	Midnight
First Quarter Moon	Full Moon	Last Quarter Moon	Dark Moon
Spring	Summer	Autumn	Winter
A Blue Circle	A Red Triangle	A Silver Crescent	A Yellow Square
The Sword	The Wand	The Cup	The Pentacle
Sylphs	Salamanders	Undines	Gnomes
The Principle Of Agency	The Generative Principle	The Principle Of Process	The Principle Of Formation
The Lesser Positive Polarity	The Greater Positive Polarity	The Greater Negative Polarity	The Lesser Negative Polarity
The Power To Know	The Power To Will	The Power To Dare	The Power To Be Silent

chart. Through ritual, meditation, and life experience a person gains the instrumentality needed to develop the part of their Self that is of that Element. In the loose sense of the word, they take the initiation of that Element. After developing each inner reflection of the Elements and expressing that development through outward changes in their personality and in their life, a person learns to keep them in balance. In some Traditions, it is said that the person then has command of the Elements. I think it is a bit more accurate to say that they have attained that which is their own power and have gained the capacity to influence that which resonates to some part of themselves. That ability to influence comes from the capacity to consciously change themselves enough to form a linkage to an external manifestation of the Elements.

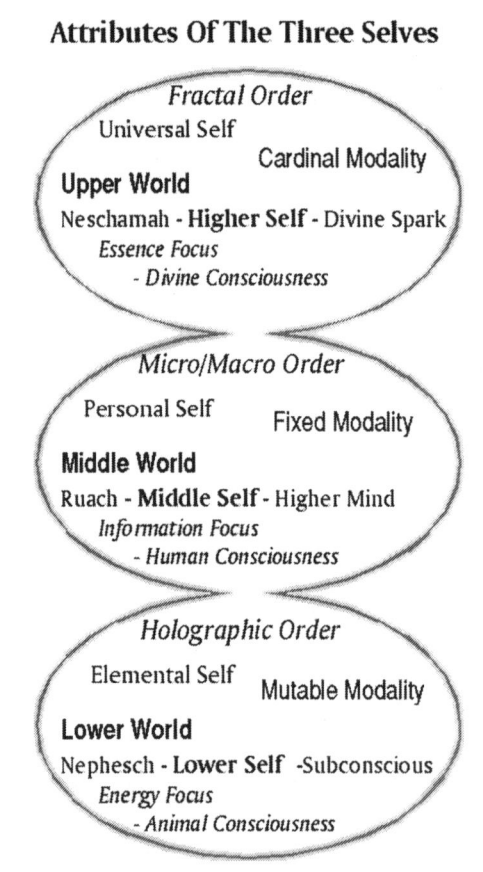

Attributes Of The Three Selves

Fractal Order
Universal Self
Cardinal Modality
Upper World
Neschamah - **Higher Self** - Divine Spark
Essence Focus
- Divine Consciousness

Micro/Macro Order
Personal Self
Fixed Modality
Middle World
Ruach - **Middle Self** - Higher Mind
Information Focus
- Human Consciousness

Holographic Order
Elemental Self
Mutable Modality
Lower World
Nephesch - **Lower Self** - Subconscious
Energy Focus
- Animal Consciousness

Many Traditions also use the concept of the Self existing in different forms on the various worlds or Planes of Being. The most prevalent simple pattern for this concept is that of the Lower, Middle, and the Higher Self (see figure on next page). If the system that you use defines more than three primary Parts of Self related to the Planes of Being, the comments that follow still apply with only minor modifications.

From the standpoint of building flexibility in the subtle bodies, it is necessary to marry together the work of the Elements and the Three Selves. One way to conceptualize this is to consider the Elements as acting on a horizontal axis and the Three Selves as acting on a vertical axis. It then becomes very evident that the Elements must be explored and understood in each of the Three Selves. Likewise, the Three Selves are best integrated by bringing the Elements into strength and balance at the level that each of the Selves operates. In a program for physical development, the muscles

Preparations And Interventions For Higher Order Workings

are worked in functional groupings; think of this as similar to working the Elements. Furthermore, care is taken to ensure that there is a balanced development of the lower body, the middle, and the upper body; this is easy to re-vision as the Three Selves. Whether viewed as the Elements or the Three Selves, working with the Parts of Self also means working with emotional, psychological, and spiritual issues that interact with each other in complicated ways. An image that captures these intricacies is that of three dimensional chess.

Although in many well developed systems of magickal practice the final outcome of following their program with discipline and vigor will be a balanced development of the Elements and the Selves, this goal is rarely stated explicitly. It is also true that systems of magickal practice, just like individuals, will tend to place greater emphasis and value on certain Parts of Self resulting in underdevelopment of others.

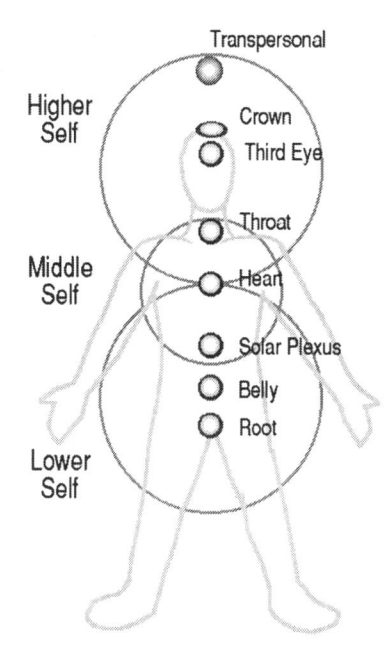

Peace, integration, and balance between the various Parts of Self is the primary source of *flexibility*. When there is cohesion and strength of identity it is possible to stretch without breaking. When there is deep integration of identity it is possible to take on a shape that is not your own without fear of losing your original form. More importantly, there is an openness, perhaps a hopeful anticipation, to the possibility of taking on a new form.

The Central Column Of Energy

The life force in our blood needs arteries, capillaries, and veins to complete its circuit. The life force that flows in our subtle bodies also uses channels to complete their circuits but those channels are of subtle matter and lines of force. In addition to the flow of subtle energy in and out from a chakra there is a flow of energy that runs from chakra to chakra up the Central Column. This flow starts beneath the feet, moves from the Root to the Crown, and is then fountained through the Transpersonal chakra into an arc that encircles the body and reenters at the feet. The Central Column of energy that connects the chakras focuses this flow of energy and is the source of polarity in human energy field. It also contains at its center an area of zero polarity much like the eye of a hurricane.

The quantity and the quality of the flow through the Central Column is first determined by the health and preparedness of the Chakras and the Parts of Self. Energy is processed, enters and exits, through the chakras and is modified by the integration of the Parts of Self before reaching the Central Column. Therefore, energetic, physical, and psychological matters must be addressed first before significant progress can be made with the Central Column. The primary factors that affect the Central Column are spiritual ones. How closely does a person align themselves with their life purposes? Do they recognize their life purposes? What is their relationship to their concept of the Divine? How much agreement and cooperation is their between their lower will and their higher will? These and all the related questions and quests that arise from these beginning points are the work of improving flow.

Some readers may be thinking that if spiritual health and spiritual development are causally related to flow, then shouldn't the focus be on spirituality first? While it is true that our spirituality is our source for guidance and inner wisdom, it does not do the work for us. The quiet voice within may offer spiritual hope, courage, and insight but nothing is changed until we change. We incarnate, participate in the world, and return through death to the realms of spirit made deeper and fuller by the experience. Similarly, there is a smaller cycle of spirit and matter within this larger one that applies here. We look to our spirituality for guidance, we apply that guidance, and the next time we look to our spirituality we do so with deeper sight and the small cycle begins again. Meditation, prayer, and magickal methods such as Middle Pillar exercises can help this process but only your efforts will smooth the path that you walk. I strongly recommend Israel Regardie's works on the Middle Pillar.

Constriction, resistance, and turbulence describe the most common symptoms associated with problems in the flow of the Central Column. Constrictions may occur in the chakras, between the parts of self, and even in the Central Column itself. The causes of constriction are many; among them a fear of being open, mistrust of the Divine, or a sense of not being worthy to receive the gift of energy from the universe. Constriction chiefly limits the volume of energy through the Central Column. Resistance's many faces include ambivalence of intent, indecision, and self-defeat. Resistance tends to limit the volume and the speed of flow by generating a sort of friction that causes discomfort and ultimately damage. Turbulence is generated when rigid energy patterns rooted in physical, emotional, or psychological problems protrude into the Central Column. Like stones and boulders in a river, these crystallized/encysted patterns, cause swirls and backwashes that interfere with the flow in chaotic ways. Turbulence has an impact on velocity, frequency, and interferes with the control of energy exiting the Central Column.

The state of the Central Column of energy is the final arbiter of *flow*. The amount and the characteristics of that flow is a very direct indication of the state of a person's spirituality. This capacity for flow is like a flower upheld and fed by the physical, psychological, and energetic strength of the person. The beauty and vigor of the bloom is in part inherent to the nature of the plant and to an equal or larger part the creation of the growth of the plant.

Emerald Heart Technique

No one technique is a full and balanced workout, but this one does a good job of encouraging *strength*, *flexibility*, and *flow* in the subtle bodies. I originally developed it in 1995 as a warming up exercise for some particularly strenuous rituals, but I have found it to be equally effective as a conditioning exercise. The name of the technique is an allusion to the Emerald Tablet of Hermes, the mechanisms of action for this method, and its impact upon the user. If you can become comfortable with holding yourself within the construct of this technique it can also be used while you are in a ritual to increase the connection between the higher heart and the higher mind. As a conditioning tool it should be used about once a week in conjunction with whatever daily practices you choose. Just as in physical exercise, if you are not doing some significant work regularly there will be no progress.

Step 1

Stand if you can, but if you must sit keep your spine as straight as possible. Become fully aware of your physical body. Focus on all the sensations and the sounds of your body. Feel the motion of your breath and the pulse of your blood. Continue until you feel fully present in your physical form. Close your eyes and stretch your consciousness so that you become distinctly aware of the shape of your body and the boundary of the skin. When the perception of your shape has become clear and distinct, move most of your consciousness inwards, leaving some of your consciousness at the surface of your body. Bring the bulk of your consciousness into focus as a sphere of emerald brilliance in the place between your breasts that is the fountainhead of the Heart Chakra.

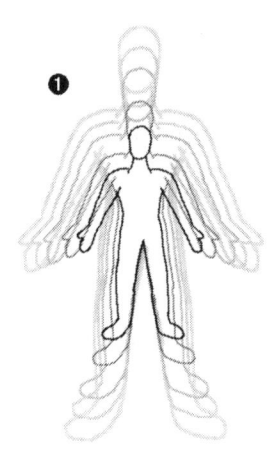

Then expand your perceptions outwards, while keeping your consciousness primarily at the Heart Chakra, and become aware of your subtle bodies. You are not moving the focus of your consciousness; you are only opening your perceptions. Take a deep breath and tone "Ahhh" and see an outflow of emerald green energy expanding your innermost subtle body. Breathe and tone for three more expansions, seeing the bodies nested within each other. It may take more than one breath for each expansion. Any pitch that your voice finds comfortable will do, but start low enough so that you can go slightly higher each time. If you can't or don't want to tone, see the green energy become bluer with each expansion.

Step 2

Envision an oval shaped sheath of brilliance that encloses all the subtle bodies that you have brought into awareness and expanded. This oval of brilliance may begin as pure white but strive for energy that is gold, aqua, or turquoise in hue. Weave this sheath of brilliance together from the energy of the universe that is outside of you. Do not create it from energy that you draw from your own center. Make certain that this enclosing oval is not opaque, it should be like a living membrane that is selective in what enters and exits. Charge it with the intent of maintaining healthy boundaries and keeping you properly energized.

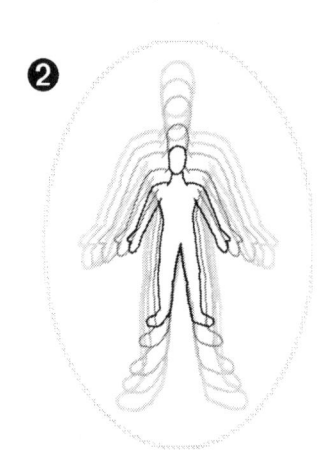

Make certain that the entire oval is equally

Preparations And Interventions For Higher Order Workings

bright and it reaches some distance below and above your most expanded subtle body. When your inspection and adjustments are complete, proceed to the next step.

Step 3

Make the oval shaped sheath contract inwards, compressing the subtle bodies towards the physical. The emerald brilliance of your Heart Chakra is like a sun whose gravity is pulling upon the layers of your subtle bodies. Take as much time as you need in doing this step. If you feel a jab of pain or uncomfortable pressure, stop and see if the discomfort passes. If the distress does not pass, slowly expand the subtle bodies and skip to step four. Depending upon the state of energetic fitness, this may take a few efforts before you succeed.

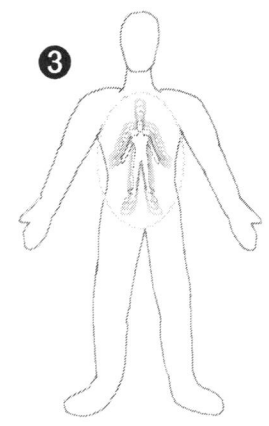

As you pull inwards, the layers of your subtle bodies that you have expanded should not merge— some space must be left between the layers. It will become harder and harder to continue as more of the layers pass through the boundary of your skin. Stop when the oval fits completely within your torso. Your sense of center of consciousness will shift and there may be a change in the color of the Heart Chakra area.

Maintain the construct through visualization and by refocusing the pull of your center of consciousness and proceed with your work. It is more effective as a conditioning exercise if you either physically walk around or cast about with your psychic senses. You will find it easier to hold the construct of the Emerald Heart within a cast circle or some other form of sacred space but it will be less effective as a conditioning tool.

Step 4

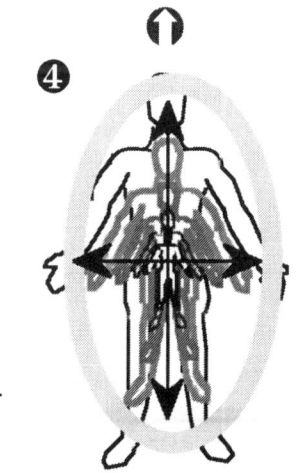

To release this working expand the oval sheath outwards by an outflow of emerald green energy from your Heart Chakra. This may be done silently or you may tone again. Continue the expansion until the oval sheath of brilliance and the layers of your subtle bodies are as expanded as they were earlier. They should all grow fainter as they expand. Then release the energy of the oval sheath back into the flux of the universe. Adjust your perceptions and intentions so that you are no longer consciously influencing the shape and size of your subtle bodies. Ground and center and allow yourself to return to your normal mode of consciousness.

Additional Information

The Emerald Heart technique does not compress the totality of your subtle bodies into the space of your physical form. It transports some portion of the higher vibration bodies into contact with lower, denser, bodies and in so doing raises the vibration of the whole by excitation. The Emerald Heart technique also overlays some amount of the higher chakras functions onto the lower chakras which raises consciousness and perception. For many people this results in their Heart Chakra seeing through the lens of the Crown or Brow Chakra. In some respects this technique resembles the Assumption of God-Forms, but instead of calling one of the Great Ones you call your Higher Self. It is strenuous and effective and therefore should be approached slowly and methodically so that you do not incur an injury by overstraining.

Interventions

Before engaging in an intervention, be aware that any intervention means becoming involved in someone's life. There is a karmic component to all interventions and it is possible to become entangled in a chain of events that would otherwise not have been a part of your life. When it is an intervention related to spiritual or magickal practices there are more layers of meaning and interaction. Whether or not this is a positive or a negative experience depends as much upon your intentions as it does upon the outcomes of your actions. Be aware in addition to your actions and those of the other person, that there are often the actions and intentions of the spirits present in the ritual to be considered. Always tend to yourself and listen for guidance before taking action. If you are not functioning out of your true will and your center, you are more likely to make regrettable choices.

Preparations And Interventions For Higher Order Workings

When To Intervene

After a powerful ritual or working it is not uncommon for a significant number of the participants to take some time to fully close down their psychic centers and return to normal. Depending upon the nature of the ritual and the emotionalpsychological state of the individual there may be outbursts of energy and/or emotion associated with the ritual. It is important to help those that are having difficulties in returning fully to the here and now. It is equally important that you allow people to complete their own process— which you may interrupt if you drag them back to normal consciousness too quickly. It is important to allow others to have their own experience. Magick, ritual, and ceremony can encourage healing and spiritual evolution. Often healing and growth are not without a certain amount of turmoil and discomfort. It would be more than a shame to help someone get stuck again after having a breakthrough in ritual.

So when do you intervene? First, ask yourself it is your role or your duty to intervene? This is more than a question of ritual etiquette, as matters can become very complicated when the energy of different interventions interact. Moreover, these unpredictable combinations can spin out of control and may disrupt the integrity of the ritual in a way that brings harm to more people. There is also the potential to damage the relationships of individuals, groups, and traditions by rash deeds which can have long lasting repercussions. It is also true that there are times when you must act, even if you are neither authorized nor designated to do so. In those rare instances, you must be very sure that your judgment and capabilities are greater than that of those who are present and that you are willing to face the consequences of seizing control. Weigh this scenario in your mind and you will find that it is your ego that often tips the scale in taking this course. The ego is often wrong.

If you are in a position to intervene, make sure that assessments and interventions occur as needed. This may be post-ritual or it may be during the ritual. If you have a hand in instructing the participants, encourage them to ground, center, and attend to their own balance of consciousness. This gives people an opportunity to take care of themselves first which is preferable. It is more likely that if people are taking care of themselves that severe reactions can be avoided or reduced in duration. Furthermore, there are more opportunities for learning when a person takes responsibility for themselves.

Assessments

Observe people carefully and when possible, *take your time* to reach your conclusions. A little clumsiness in moving or unsteadiness is normal for many people. Giddiness or tears are also within the range of safety. If a person is acting in a manner disruptive during a ritual, determine why they are being disruptive before acting. It may appear that they have lost their focus and are joking and laughing, but it may also be hysteria or the beginning of some trance state. It can be very jarring and ungrounding to be scolded or hushed if the disruptive behavior comes from being in an altered state of consciousness. It takes careful work to intervene during a ritual in a manner that is helpful to all involved. An intervention should not cause a greater disruption than the one that it is meant to correct. After a ritual, pay close attention to anyone who is not taking an active part in normal post-ritual social interaction. Hugs, handshakes, well wishing, and exchanges of kisses of fellowship encourage grounding as well as integration of the ritual experience into mundane life. If a person is not taking part in these activities it may indicate that they are caught up in their internal emotional process or are so ungrounded as to make these actions difficult. In and of itself this is not a good enough reason to do anything more than continuing your observations and assessments.

In the case of people that you know, it should be fairly easy to spot behavior that is out of their norm. In a public ritual there will be strangers present and assessing them will be more difficult. If people are not participating in post ritual closing activities watch the flow of expressions on their face. If you can see that they are actively observing the other people and appear to be taking in the experience, then in all likelihood they are fine. You may wish to check in with them just to make sure they feel included. If a person whom you do not know has a vacant or an odd expression on their face, check with your friends to see if anyone knows the person in question. They may have a sense of what is normal for that person. Some people do not like to hug after a ritual or need some quiet time to complete their closing down process. If there is a problem, a familiar face as part of the intervention is useful. If you can see auras or if someone in your group can see auras, then check out the person's energy. Once again it is better if the person doing the psychic assessment knows what is normal for an individual as there is a great deal of variation in people's auras. There is no real substitute for second sight in making assessments, but your physical senses can tell you quite a bit.

Regardless of all other indications, if a person goes from a standing to a

Preparations And Interventions For Higher Order Workings

sitting position or fails to get up after a ritual you should approach them immediately. Do not create an air of crisis or drama in making the approach, and don't forget to take that stern, serious, or alarmed expression off your face first. The difficulty may be something as commonplace as an aching back or bad knees that need to be moved with care. If a person tells you that they are fine take them at their word, but keep an eye on them from a distance. Sometimes bad responses to ritual take time to fully develop. The damage or strain will have occurred in subtle bodies that operate on planes of being where time operates differently and hence will manifest in linear time in accordance with the rules that govern the propagation of actions from plane to plane. In most cases, the person may need help anywhere from ten minutes to an hour after the ritual. Other effects may make themselves known later, but severe responses tend to have a quick onset. Whenever possible get the opinion of another knowledgeable person in your group. You will have just been in ritual yourself and will not have your full faculties or complete clarity. Your judgment should be counterbalanced by another's perceptions. Even in unmistakably prominent instances, or when the person seeks you out for help, it is still important to get a second opinion.

If indeed you determine that the person needs some type of magickal assistance, assess their training and background first. If the person is a novice there is a high probability that they merely need to be talked through grounding with perhaps some energy assistance. Often the reaction seems more pronounced because it is a new experience for the individual. Remember also that sometimes an old hand is also a novice in some ways. A person may come from a tradition or a path that is very spiritually developed but with relatively little magickal experience. Also a strong faith or religious background, of itself, does not prepare a person for spirit contact or the energetic atmospheres generated by rituals with a magickal focus. If the person is experienced and they are having a difficult time, there is a strong possibility that the situation is more serious. Sometimes the reaction is not related so much in response to the ritual as it is to the shock or surprise of experiencing something that proves the existence of something outside of their world view. The awe of experiencing something that proves their faith can also push a person to the edge of panic.

There is a tendency to assume that an adverse reaction is rooted in the magick, and often the emotional component is primary and the magick is incidental. If you determine that the person's primary need is emotional support while processing the experience, ask them what they want. You may offer or be asked to hold them, let them cry, listen to them, etc... Simply be fully focused on them, giving unconditional positive regard, and let them give full expression to their emotions. Be aware that ritual tends to stir people deeply and that the emotions that rise to the surface may have their origins outside the ritual. Moreover many people experience increased empathy in ritual space and may have their feelings modulated by those of the others who are present. After a bit it may be appropriate to suggest that you can go to a more comfortable place, and/or to get something to eat or drink. You may encourage them to write down what they are thinking and feeling, or have someone write it down for them, so that they can consider the themes raised when they have regained their balance. The promise that it will be attended to later often makes it easier to release the emotions fully.

It almost goes without saying that you should ascertain whether or not a medical condition is not the primary cause of a person's difficulty. Blood sugar levels and blood pressure, in particular, tend to be strongly affected by some rituals. If in addition to a physical problem, the person is also ungrounded, they may not remember to tell you that they have a medical condition. Ask them directly if they have any medical condition and if they are on any medications. If the person is not able to answer coherently, pull in another person (preferably one with a health care background) and determine whether or not emergency medical help is needed. There is an understandable reluctance to call outsiders to the site of a ritual, but if it is a medical matter, appropriate care must be summoned or the person must be taken to the care.

Remain Calm, Centered, & Clear

It is common sense that you need to remain calm, centered, and clear in order to help someone else. It isn't necessarily easy to do so. Severe reactions are rare, but they do happen. Don't become complacent or believe that you are an authority on these things just because you've seen a few ungrounded people. Severe reactions will always be frightening no matter how often you have seen them. Like most emergency situations, you will not have weathered it before the actual incident. You can somewhat reduce your reaction by desensitizing yourself through visualizations of possible scenarios. Take some time to visualize what it would be like to see someone's eyes roll back into their head; see them drenched in sweat and shaking. Imagine a person not responding to their name or believing that they are in a different time or place.

It is also helpful to have a method to quickly achieve a clear and focused state of being for yourself. Find a relaxation or meditation technique that works for you and do it until it is automatic. Do it until a single word or image is enough to key you into that state of being— emulate Pavlov's dogs.

Determining What Is Needed

The process of checking in with the person, interpreting your psychic perceptions, and consulting with your colleagues will in most cases lead to a clear course of actions. If you have spiritual beings (patrons, guides, higher self, etc.) that you work with you will wish their input as well. If it is possible for you to connect with the higher self of the person in crisis, all the better. Before beginning make a prayer or an affirmation to ask for Divine help by whatever names you use. If you know something of what the person's belief system may be, offer a prayer and a request for assistance from their tradition as well. Sometimes a person will tell you what they believe is wrong and will suggest what needs to be done. Their self-assesment may or may not be accurate. They may not have the training to understand their situation or they may be to befuddled to come to sound conclusions. Take in what they offer as one more piece of information to be considered with the rest. It may also be the case that their faith, religion, or personal preferences require that the help be given by a person of a specific gender, faith, or within certain guidelines. Depending upon the circumstances, the person may or may not give consent to receive assistance. To intervene without consent opens up an abyss of ethical and karmic complications. If the person is incoherent unconscious, listen for inner guidance, apply the strength of your cognitive powers, then do what you feel is best, knowing the gravity of that choice.

Please Don't!

The following is a list of common mistakes:

• Do not infuse the person with any additional energy. This includes systems such as Reiki that some claim to be harmless in all settings. Healing methods, formal or informal, that most people use tend to aggravate severe ritual reactions. In some cases there will be temporary relief purchased with a future cost.

• Homeopathic or Flower essences remedies are good for stabilizing a person in shock. Rescue Remedy in particular is a good choice. Even people who do not normally respond to homeopathic or flower essence remedies tend to be receptive to their benefits immediately after an energy trauma. However: If more than 3-4 hours have passed since the onset of the reaction, administering these remedies may make matters worse as they will activate layers of the subtle bodies that should be resting.

- More cooks do spoil the broth! Limit the number of people assisting to no more than three. If a more talented or more experienced person arrives on the scene, yield your space to them after passing on your impressions.

- Do not encourage a repeat performance on the part of the ungrounded individual. Do not dote on, hover over, or mother them after the crisis is over. Some people will find the attention they receive in this context to be a strong incentive to be ungrounded again. For some this will be deliberate and for others it will be an unconscious action. In either case if an individual has repeated severe reactions, a serious talk is in order about the risks these incidents pose to all who are involved.

- Don't pass the ungrounded person's energy through your aura. There are times and places when this is appropriate as in healing and in helping others to ground from mild reactions. In the case of severe reactions, the risk of being hurt by such a practice is real. Moreover the helper may become unable to provide further assistance even if they are not hurt. This is risky healing work, and you should take precautions. Remember that if you have just participated in a ritual, your subtle bodies may be tired and vulnerable to injury.

Tool Chest For Bringing Them Back

Reviving Aroma-
Mix 2 drops of Cedar oil and 2 drops of Ambergris oil in a small glass or ceramic bowl— not metal. Encourage the person to smell the mixture, and to imagine the fertile earth warming beneath the Sun's touch. Do not mix the oils before use as they react with each other during storage in a way that lessens their effect. This tool will help to shift the focus from the subtle to the physical senses.

Yarrow Florets (*Achillea millefolium*)-
One or two fresh white yarrow florets, lightly chewed and held under the tongue for no more than a minute often brings about a sudden increase in

Preparations And Interventions For Higher Order Workings

mental clarity. The person should spit out the floret when they feel clarity returning and should touch the roof of their mouth with the tip of their tongue for a moment. Dried yarrow florets can be used if they have been soaked in water before the ritual, but are somewhat less effective. You can freeze yarrow flowers to have fresher ones on hand. The white ones are the most potent for this purpose. You should ask if the person is allergic before giving them yarrow. If a person is so groggy that they could choke, do not give them yarrow. This tool attracts and redirects mental energy back into the person.

Summoning Breath-

Ask the person to become aware of their breath. Ask them to slow down their breathing. When they have controlled their breathing ask them to exhale all the air from their bodies that they can and to hold on empty for a count of three. Continue slow breathing with holding on empty, increasing the hold on empty to a count of five. This pattern of breathing summons the subtle bodies, drawing them closer to the physical body. Holding on empty helps to synchronize the rhythm of the blood, prana, and cerebrospinal fluid. If the person will not listen and is diving in and out of their body, you may need to hold their nose with your fingers. This tool will help to reconnect the subtle bodies and the various Parts of Self but will not restore a person's energy balance.

Energy Shunt-

To drain off excess energy without potentially overloading or contaminating your own aura create a thoughtform for just that purpose. Visualize a tube of blue-white energy connecting to the most inflamed part of the persons aura and see the other end of the tube plunging down deep into the earth. The excess energy should flow on its own, drawn by the differences in polarity. If the energy does not flow immediately the person is holding on to it. Ask the person to let the excess drain away. If needed, cause the tube to pulse either by visualization or by manipulating it with your hands. If the energy flow is large you may need to guide the flow with your hands, but don't touch it directly.

It Shall Be Naught-

In rituals that are more magickal than celebratory (more task oriented than devotional), loose energy and unstable intent can put the wheels of manifestation in motion in unwanted ways. If the person is agitated check in with them to see if they saw something disturbing or had disturbing thoughts. They may not feel comfortable expressing negative thoughts, imagery, or wishes. Gently, without encouraging flights of fear and fancy, suggest to them that they may wish to make an affirmation that their fear will not manifest. Modify your suggestions as needed, but the essence is to stop unwanted manifestations. In addition to blocking the unwanted, reinforce the stated intent of the ritual and ground any loose energy into that intent.

The Square Of Abeyance-
In those blessedly rare cases when the person is actually being harmed by a spirit the casting of a Square of Abeyance is a quick remedy. Once the casting is complete the person will have a moment of discomfort that should pass quickly. The discomfort may be experienced as slight respiratory distress. The Square is a powerful dampening field that closes down the psychic senses and the pathways between the planes of being. They should experience the dull heaviness of the casting for at least three full minutes after the initial discomfort before the Square is dismissed. There is a chapter in my book *Castings: The Creation Of Sacred Space on the Square*. For your convenience, I am reprinting a one page summary as an appendix in this book.

Hold Fast-
If a person's primary complaint is a sensation of floating or leaping in and out of their body, ask them if they feel relatively well while they are grounding. If they do, then determine how long they can remain grounded and centered before they lose their control or focus. This will tell you how much time you have to work. Ask them to ground, center, and to let you know when they are ready. Place the Pranic Bindrune on the crown of their head using blue-green energy, then place a Quartered Circle on the soles of both feet using yellow ochre colored energy. The symbols will dissipate on their own but should act as splints until the person's energy balance returns.

Stabilizing Them

These are techniques that can be used to keep a person here and balanced if they begin to relapse into a reaction. This assistance need not be offered by the same individual(s) that provided the initial intervention. However if the care of an individual is being passed on to others that were not part of the initial intervention, a detailed synopsis of the situation should be relayed. If you are part of the planning for a ritual that will have a large number of participants, it is good to create teams to ensure good

Preparations And Interventions For Higher Order Workings

initial contacts and follow-ups. Before using one of these stabilizing methods, try to assess the cause of the relapse. It may be that the ritual space has not been fully shut down. No methods will warm or comfort a person for long if they are still in a location where the winds are still blowing between the worlds. It may also be the case that some part of the person is leading them back into the adverse reaction. Try to name and to address any causes that you find before proceeding.

Pacemaker-

If the person's aura and chakras look washed out and they report that they feel exhausted, use this technique. Have the person lay down on their back, or if that isn't possible ask them to sit with their spine straight. Draw energy in through all five fingers of your dominant hand and focus the energy into a sphere using your palm chakra. Hold the sphere of energy over the person's chakra that you would like to affect. Use your palm chakra to adjust the color, frequency, etc. of the sphere. Continue to feed energy in through your fingers to the sphere. Do not feed energy from the sphere to the person's aura or chakras! You are manipulating the energy by resonance— not by direct contact. The presence of a focused and color specific energy pattern near the weakened chakra will encourage it to resume normal functioning without invasive measures.

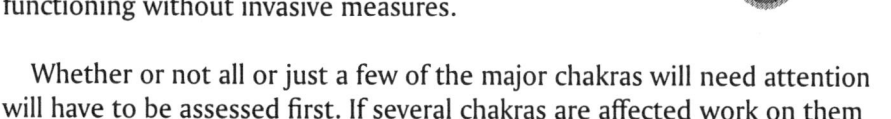

Whether or not all or just a few of the major chakras will need attention will have to be assessed first. If several chakras are affected work on them in order from root towards crown.

The alternative to this technique is Recharging The Etheric Body.

Recharging The Etheric Body-

Most commonly, the subtle body that receives the greatest stress in adverse reactions to ritual is the Etheric. This is the energy body that lies just above the physical and closely mirrors the physical form. It is this body that is caught in energy clashes and dissonances of the lower and the higher forces during an imbalance. If the person reports that they feel cold, or are still trembling, or lack fine muscle coordination, use this technique. Place a blue or purple fluorite crystal in their dominant hand and an amethyst in their non-dominant hand. Ask them to intone "Oooo, Ohhh, Oooo" in a low rumbling pitch. Check in with them and repeat until they feel better. If you don't have crystals available, have them make these tones while you make the tone "Awww" at as low a pitch as you can.

The alternative to this technique is the Pacemaker.

Name Chant-
This is a two part chant (spoken or droned) that helps to reaffirm the person's place in the here and now. The name *Judy* is used in this example.

> You chant: "Judy, You Are Here. Judy, We Are With You."
> They chant: "I Am Here. I Am Here. I Am Here".
> You repeat "Judy, You Are Here. Judy, We Are With You."

Chant until the person brings it to a close.

Sealing The Portals-
After a physical shock to the system, oftentimes it is necessary to wrap someone in a blanket or move them to a cool shady spot because their body has a hard time maintaining a steady temperature. Outside changes in the environment that normally would pose no challenge become daunting tasks. After a shock to the subtle bodies from the impact of the energy raised in ritual or the pressure of the consciousness of spirits, the chakras and other subtle portals can become sluggish in responding to the energy environment. Often this manifests as being locked in the open position which leaves them vulnerable to further energy imbalance and spiritual disturbance. Whenever possible, encourage the person through a simple visualization to close each of the major chakras starting at the top and working your way down. It is better if they do this work themselves. If they are not able to do this, help them using your hand moving in a slow counterclockwise motion above each chakra. There is a minor chakra, but a critically important one, that should be attended to after the major chakras have been closed down. This minor chakra is located at the nape of the neck which is the back of the neck where it joins the torso. It is the portal through which many people connect to the consciousness of nonphysical beings. Even if all the major chakras are closed, when the nape chakra is open, people can lose clarity of consciousness or worse because of spiritual presences.

Food & Drink-
Often people in the throes of a reaction will not have any desire for food and drink. Coax the person into eating or drinking something that is sweet, unless diabetes or other conditions make this inadvisable. As soon as possible after the sweet treat, get the person to eat a small quantity of something rich in protein. High protein food is harder to digest which redirects

the person's energy into their body. Moreover, high protein food will help adjust brain chemistry in the direction of normal beta wave consciousness. Less commonly, some people will crave large quantities of sweets (including fruit and other natural sources of fast burning sugars). A small quantity of sugar may be useful, large doses will generate further problems. Chocolate is a good choice for many people— in a small dose.

The Ontogeny Sigil-

If there is significant identity confusion and especially if the person has been Aspecting, Drawing Down, etc., and other methods have not worked then the Ontogeny Sigil should be used. Have the person sit in a comfortable position and give them the Ontogeny Sigil and ask them to look at its center. Scribe a circle around them using blue-green energy that encloses them and them alone. Stand in a circle around the scribed one and chant: "Ahhh-Liiihh-Tawhnn" Let the "nn" sound hang in the air before each repetition. Continue chanting until they indicate that it is enough. See the appendix on using the Ontogeny Sigil for further instructions.

Stronger Measures?

If these suggestions are not sufficient, then serious work is needed that falls outside the reach of a single chapter. This work may entail healing rituals, psychological therapy, conditioning of the subtle bodies, and prayer. Shamanic methods such as Soul Retrieval, energetic healing to reweave the auric shell, rituals of cleansing, or ceremonial magick rituals based on the Isis-Osiris myth cycle are among the many possibilities to be pursued. The one certainty is that only exceptionally talented and rigorously trained practitioners should be engaging in this difficult and perilous work.

Knowing Your Limits

Take care of yourself in your role as a helper. When offering assistance make sure that you have made full use of the support and resources available in your fellow magickal workers. Know yourself and the boundaries of your capabilities so that you will be ready to refrain from intervening when you are not the best choice. Know the wisdom of referral. Also, when the manner or the mode of a person's adverse ritual reaction makes you afraid, disgusted, angry, or in some way presses in on your personal fears or weaknesses, see if someone else is available to handle the matter. There is no shame in knowing your limits, or pushing beyond them when the need arises. If you do indeed find that you have exceeded your limits because of an urgent need, make sure that you receive support and help once the crisis has passed.

Remember that you are the greatest resource that you draw upon to do spiritual work. Treat yourself like the treasure that you are.

Mediumship, Channeling, & Mediation

Lacking a commonly agreed upon set of definitions, discussions of channeling and mediumship in the general metaphysical community can be a bit confusing. Many established systems and traditions use these terms very differently and because there are genuine similarities between the various practices, the confusion can be compounded by the illusion of agreement. It is not so much that the divisions between these practices is arbitrary as it is that different systems will draw the lines in those places that match their perspectives and their sensibilities. What I share in this chapter is the set of lines, boxes, and connecting arrows that I use to give a useful order to what I know of mediumship, channeling, and mediation. Mediation is a term that is used by a relatively small portion of systems in the broader Western Magickal Tradition to describe practices that blend the high end of channeling and mediumship. I include it here because, as you'll see, it serves to resolve the distinctions between channeling and mediumship.

Mediumship, channeling, and mediation all arise from the use of both psychism and magick in varying proportions according to their context. In order to define and discuss mediumship, channeling, and mediation it is necessary to explore the different contributions made by psychism and magick to these practices.

Psychism

For the most part psychism is understood to be those sensory inputs that are derived from a conscious connection to the ethereal organs of perception in the subtle bodies. These subtle senses are often named after the physical sense that they most resemble such as clairaudience which derives from the French word for *light* and the Latin word for *hearing*. The derivation of the word is very apt because a person engaging in clairaudience is indeed hearing light. The *clairs*, as I like to call them, are the dominant form of psychism. All the clairs involve a routing of subtle perceptions through the mechanisms that are used in physical perceptions in order to bring them into conscious awareness. In this form of psychism, people see, hear, smell, taste, and feel those things that have no substance. Less commonly, psychism can also take a different route for expression. A modification of the boundaries and the volitional structures that exist between the conscious and the preconscious can also result in psychic perception and communication. Automatic writing, automatic drawing/painting speaking in trance, and other kinds of communicative actions that occur without apparent thought or volition belong to this other form of psychism. I call these the *noirs*, the darks in contrast to the clairs. Each person has within themselves a multitude of preprogrammed subroutines that facilitate daily life and can be invoked by the slightest act of will. Assuming no illness or disability, it takes very little effort or thought to turn the pages of this book . You do not pause to think of each muscle filament that must contract or relax or of the sequence of myriad and minute actions that are triggered by your command to turn the page. You will it — and it is so. If the individual, and those structures related to their will, step aside, and leave open the access route to the controls that activate those preprogrammed actions, this other family of psychic abilities presents itself. Although in the past it was more common for mediums to rely primarily on the *noirs* and for channelers to rely primarily on the *clairs* for their work, this is not the case anymore. Regardless of the type of psychism used, psychism is the primary vehicle for communication used in channeling, mediumship, and mediation. The starting values for the quality and the attributes of those communications are set by the caliber of the practitioner's psychism. An important point that figures later in this chapter is the difference between how information is conveyed to the medium or channeler's consciousness in these two categories of psychism.

Magick

There are many forms and styles of magick, so I will only focus on its uses for the purposes at hand. Magick as it is applied in channeling, mediumship, and mediation is the use of symbolic actions that connect the practitioner to a conceptual framework that is larger than the practitioner and the spirits with whom they have interactions. These symbolic actions may be as simple as the lighting of a candle and the offering of a prayer or may be full blown multilayered rituals. Magick acts to refine and to augment the effectiveness of whatever type of psychism is being used. It does so by stabilizing the communication through the pre-filtering and the pre-processing that comes from the context created by the world view that is embedded in the magick. This context is partly psychological but just as importantly it is also the energetic structures that exist on the other planes of being that arise from the tradition and the history of the magick that is employed. For some practitioners there is considerable overlap between their concept of magick and their concept of religion. For others, magick and religion are very separate things indeed, but relative to their use in channeling, mediumship, and mediation the results are in essence one.

As was noted earlier, the starting values of the communications may be derived by the characteristics of the practitioner, but these can be greatly modified through the use of magick. The energetic structures, that are external to the practitioner that ceremony and ritual provide, can offer assistance that is comparable to some common tools that humans use. These structures can be: like reading glasses that bring things into focus, like an external antenna that brings a stronger signal into the receiver, or like the comfort of a house that allows a sense of security that facilitates clear thinking.

Joined together, psychism and magick provide the raw materials and tools that allow for the construction of those things that we call mediumship, channeling, and mediation. It may be useful to view these three practices as three different houses. The materials and tools to build them may have been the same at the beginning, but the plans and the execution of those plans makes all the difference.

Mediumship

The term mediumship reveals something of the nature of the practice. A medium is very much like an artist's medium, they are the paint that is put onto the canvas. They are also like the air, a medium that carries and makes possible what we call sound and speech. In mediumship the person's psychism and their physical form is made available for the spirits to use in order to express themselves. As was brought up in the first chapter, contact with nonphysical beings contains varying proportions of energy, information, and essence. The spirits of the dead with which mediums generally communicate have very limited stores of energy to draw upon. A talented medium will disengage most of their volitional attachment to the mechanisms of perception and/or motion and also ramp up the sensitivity of the triggers for those mechanisms. Imagine for a moment that the medium is like a keyboard and that the spirit is trying to push those keys. Given their insubstantial state and their limited access to denser energy, they are more likely to be successful if it only requires the lightest, briefest, touch to actuate the keys. The bulk of what is conveyed through a medium is information, with some small amount of essence to provide the seed for understanding.

Those of you familiar with mediumship and the lore of contact with spirits may beg to differ on the score of how much energy a spirit can have or on its capacity to impact upon the physical world. There are numerous well documented cases of moving objects and manifestations tied to ghostly activity. I have had personal experiences of such things. One autumn night, with all the windows closed, we had a wind chime inside our house ring loudly enough to wake us. When I went to investigate, it was still ringing and swinging back and forth. We discovered a day later that a friend had died when his lover called to make arrangements to scatter his ashes in the memorial circle in our woods. I have no argument connecting spiritual presences with palpable, physical occurrences, but the source of the energy is not the spirits, rather it is the humans with whom they interact. In the case of our friend who announced his passing at our house, his spirit had numerous sources of vital energy. He was the High Priest of a coven whose energy he could draw upon. The wind chime that rang hangs above an altar in the North-East part of our house that is our *designated* portal for spirits to enter and this altar is keyed to our energy. This explains why readings, sessions with mediums, are often more successful with a group of willing people because of the availability of energy to drive the process.

Mediums who have the capacity for producing manifestations are rare, but then so are people that have significant psychokinetic ability. This is not an inconsequential connection. It is often true that those mediums that bring through powerful manifestations don't exhibit signs of active psychism or magickal power that matches their mediumistic ability. All of us have the potential for many gifts and talents that we never awaken. In the case of psychokinesis and active magickal powers, psychology comes to bear in that we generally only allow ourselves as much power as we think we deserve or as we trust ourselves to use well. If a medium has these rare talents it is just as likely that they are unaware of them, afraid of them, or has shut them down or out. When a medium metaphorically steps out of the way, the visiting spirit may use whatever resources it finds at its disposal whether or not the owner of those resources would do so. There are some exceptions to these general parameters about energy, manifestations, and mediumship that are clarified in the chapter "Ghosts & Ancestors".

Although it may sound paradoxical to some ears, the receptivity that is required for mediumship to function well is not passive. In fact one of the characteristics that distinguishes between the grades of mediumship is the amount of active engagement in the management of the receptive state. A medium at the lower end of development may expend most of their effort on quieting the mind and disengaging from the mechanisms of their body. In this state they are open and sensitive but not very selective or focused. They may or may not make contact with the spirit that is being sought. They may bring through something but it may be thoughts or information from the loudest living minds present or whatever presence is near. At this stage of development, the act of trying to seek a particular spirit or to focus the communication drops them out of their receptive state. Like a juggler, over time they develop the skill needed to juggle more and more balls simultaneously. Some individuals have enough reserve mental capacity so that they are able to allocate more consciousness and cognition to the tasks of refining the communication than others. This mental capacity is a separate talent from whatever psychism the individual may have.

One of the techniques used to manage the receptivity of a medium is the use of a *control*. In Spiritualist literature, the control is a spirit that acts in the role of the go-between, the handler, and the broker between the medium and spirits that would communicate through the medium. In truth, the control is rarely a spirit. There are very few spirits who have the availability and the inclination to take on the task of managing a medium. The control is almost always some portion of the medium's consciousness that has been partitioned into a separate functioning unit. This is also true of many of the *guides* that people have as well. This dissociated portion of Self is comparable in many ways to the magickal personality/persona of Ceremonial Magick or of the fetch, double, or co-walker of certain forms of Witchcraft. For a variety of psychological and metaphysical reasons, this externalization and personification of a separate focus of attention and cognition is the most expedient solution to the task of maintaining an active and adaptive receptivity. Although ultimately for the health and spiritual development of the medium integration rather than dissociation is preferable, the work to achieve such development may, in many cases, be outside of the reach of what an individual can accomplish in one lifetime. Most commonly, a medium's progression in their work involves a change in which a portion of Self is given the task of being the control or the guide. It should be noted that for some mediums questions posed to the spirit are passed through the control and that for others the questions are deposited by the medium directly at the boundary between the conscious and the preconscious.

Our consciousness, our being, exists on multiple planes simultaneously. In truth our *being* is a continuum with no gaps, but like the rainbow, there are segments that we identify as particular colors. Just as there are many names for the colors, different Traditions use different names and boundaries for these colors of consciousness. For the sake of simplicity, let us use the terms Lower, Middle, and Higher Self. A beginning medium who has progressed far enough to have established some type of control or guide generally creates it out of their Lower Self. I should point out at this time that many never get beyond this point because they become enamored of the process and its *glamour*. Those that progress to the place of drawing upon their Middle Self often experience a temporary diminishment of their mediumistic skills unless they have also done work that develops the higher mind in which case there is greater clarity. There is the potential for greater interference from the medium's emotions, attachments, prejudices, and beliefs as these are closely connected to the personality that resides in the Middle Self. There is also a change in the nature of consciousness at this level which requires adjustments. These are growing pains and some choose to regress rather than to pass through them. If the medium progresses to the point of drawing upon their Higher Self as their guide, then the quality and the specificity of their communication is only limited by their personal level of evolution and that of the spirit that they contact.

Aside from the question of which level of the Self is functioning as the control, much of the variation in the styles and capacities of mediums arise from each individual's unique profile of psychic gifts. The most notable factor in these profiles is the ratio between their clairs and their noirs. On the surface, those mediums that have a preponderance of noirs will appear to function in the classic style of mediumship. Those mediums that have a preponderance of clairs often appear to be practicing in a manner that resembles channeling except that the focus is communication with the dead. Despite appearances, mediumship is not channeling. These two divergent expressions of mediumship have in common the foundation of receptivity. The medium does not travel to the spirit, this is not an kinetic pursuit. Some may disagree with this perspective, saying that high order mediums travel on the Astral. I would say that it is more accurate to say that the medium shifts their focus of attention. We exist, through our subtle bodies, on many planes of being at once, the Astral being one of them. If I am holding two objects, one in each hand, and I shift my focus of attention from one hand to the other to feel the shapes of the objects, I have not traveled though something has moved. The medium draws the spirit to the time and the place of the reading, almost like a magnet or a beacon by offering their receptivity. Communication occurs through the instrument of the medium's storehouse of automated responses. This is also true in the case of the medium that relies primarily on the clairs such as clairvoyance or clairaudience. Our sensory and perceptual capacities are also highly automated. All of the sensory data that we subjectively experience *as the world* has been preprocessed in countless ways before it reaches our waking consciousness.

Whether it is speaking in trance, automatic writing, or an internal dialogue, medium experiences the information as coming from an external source. Their waking consciousness then tries to make sense of the information much the way that we try to make sense of any conversation. The spirit expresses itself by using the media of the medium. Another way to look at it is that the spirit is like a visitor from a foreign land who is trying to converse with the medium by flipping through a phrase book provided by the medium.

Channeling

When we look at the words channeling or channeler, there is the implication that the person is serving as a conduit or a pipeline for the information that they convey. While it is certainly true that channelers strive to be clear and smooth conduits, it is more accurate to think of them as translators or interpreters. Whereas a medium configures themselves so that the mechanisms of communication are actuated by the spirit that they contact, the channeler uses their psychism directly and processes the information into an intelligible message. Another way of putting this is that in mediumship the spirits access the boundary between the preconscious and the conscious. In channeling, the spirits *speak* in energetic patterns that are perceived by the equivalent of sensory organs in the subtle bodies. The channel itself is actually the set of linkages that pipe these energetic patterns from the higher subtle bodies into the lower subtle bodies and ultimately into the consciousness of the channeler. Channeling is primarily an active pursuit with a counterbalance of receptivity that is the mirror image of the receptivity with a control of the medium. The words *channeling* and *mediumship* reveal the natures of the practices. Channeling ends with the *ing* that indicates that it is an action. Mediumship ends with *ship* that indicates that it is a state of being. Despite these differences, the bulk of what is conveyed through a channeler, like a medium, also is information, with some small amount of essence to provide the seed for understanding.

The channeler does travel in a manner of speaking. When a contact is sought, some portion of one of their upper subtle bodies seeks until it can find the locus where it and the spirit can maintain a stable connection. This locus can be thought of as having multiple coordinates assigned by factors such as plane of being, time frame, frequency range, and correlation to geography. The stability of the connection depends upon how taxing or how comfortable the locus is for all the parties involved. For example if the lowest plane that a spirit can hold itself at is the highest plane that a channeler can reach, the communication will be brief or quickly deteriorate. The channeler can be compared to a mountain climber that has reached too high a peak and will begin to lose lucidity unless they descend. The spirit can be likened to a diver who is swimming hard against their natural buoyancy to remain in the depths. Some channelers have a conscious awareness of journeying and others do not. Whether or not they are aware of the journey as they seek the contact is more a question of sensibilities and psychology than it is one of methods or techniques. Although the techniques and the experiences differ in many ways, there is an underlying commonality in the modes of seeking used by both channelers and shamans.

The quality of channeling is determined to a great degree by two conditions. One is the strength and coherence of the linkages between their various subtle bodies which we can call alignment. The other is the breadth and the depth of the channeler's knowledge and wisdom. All information entering the Self must pass through each subtle body before it can progress to the next subtle body. The state of each layer of the aura (subtle body) determines how much clarity will be retained or distortion added. The state of the threshold, the transition from one subtle body, to another determines how much of the message will pass or be truncated. This process holds true for both incoming and outgoing messages. The figures are highly simplified but contain the gist of what occurs. The role of the channelers knowledge and wisdom is significant because they are like translators or interpreters. If they do not have the vocabulary, and I am using this word in the broadest sense, or a wellspring of concepts to extrapolate from, it is likely that they will mistranslate or misinterpret the message that does reach their consciousness. The role of knowledge, education, and wisdom is also very important in mediumship and in mediation, but the nature of channeling make this a more critical limiting factor.

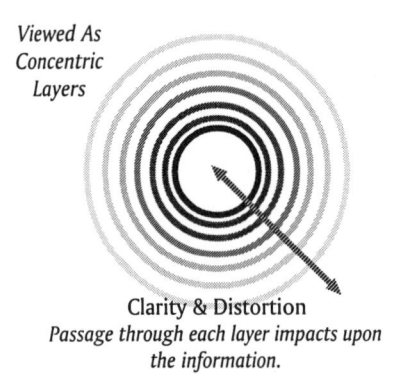

Viewed As Concentric Layers

Clarity & Distortion
Passage through each layer impacts upon the information.

Channelers, as a group, are more idiosyncratic than mediums in how

Mediumship, Channeling, & Mediation

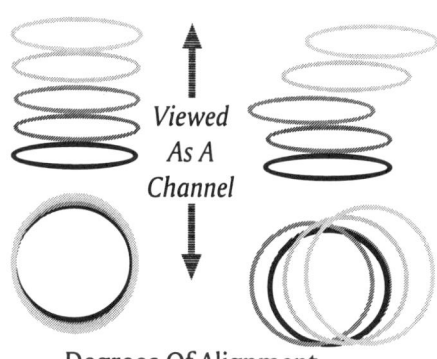

Viewed As A Channel

Degrees Of Alignment
The higher the misalignment, the greater truncation and loss.

they express their capacities. This is due to channeling involving the use of more distinct levels and portions of the Self within the channeler to create the pathways for communication. As with any system, the more components the greater the probability of variations and ranges of response. Channeling and mediumship are peers, and equal in the sense of their value, but they rule over different territories. Channeling and mediumship also draw upon different populations of individuals.

With a certain amount of psychism and training, many people can learn to channel. However even with psychism and training, very few people can learn to be mediums. There is some balance in this state of affairs. Although many can learn to channel, very few get good at it no matter how hard they try. Although few can learn to be mediums, a fairly high portion get good at it if they persevere.

As a general rule channelers are better at communication with spirits that are not human or have moved beyond the wheel of incarnation and mediums are better at communicating with spirits that are fully human. This is an outcome of the means by which they accomplish communication. A human spirit is more familiar with the actuation of the circuits in the medium. A non-human or beyond-human spirit is better able to cause and to shape the vibrations that are sensed by the channeler. Some people have the capacity for mediumship and for channeling. These dually endowed people generally have to switch gears to shift between these two modes. How smoothly this shifting occurs is a measure of their inner agility and dexterity. This transition between modes can be so smooth as to be hardly noticeable or it can be a grinding and lurching ride. In some rare individuals the capacity for mediumship and channeling can evolve into the capacity for mediation.

Mediation

I have met or sampled the work of over a hundred channelers. I have met or sampled the work of several score of mediums. I have met or sampled the work of less than a dozen mediators. There are very few mediators, so few that the term is generally unknown even in metaphysical circles. Mediators stand at the midpoint between channeling and mediumship, trance and waking consciousness, activity and passivity, and a multiplicity of other complementary pairings. Like mediums and channelers their contact is information driven but contains a much greater proportion of essence. They move in and out of the conditions needed for spirit contact with an ease and poise rarely seen in channeling or mediumship. Partly this is because mediators have a broader range of depths and intensities in their practice. Lower order mediums and channelers tend to either be on or off. More advanced ones tend to have a number of established depths and intensities to which they can click their consciousness. For mediators, within whatever their range may be, there is infinite adjustability. This shifting of consciousness can happen so swiftly and smoothly that they can interject a piece of information from the other realms into the midst of an otherwise mundane conversation without missing a beat. This fluidity of action arises from the nature of mediation.

Unlike the polarized states generated by channeling or mediumship, a mediator changes the configuration of their consciousness from one state of dynamic equilibrium to another state of dynamic equilibrium. To achieve such states requires a great deal of flexibility and a core self that is very resilient and very malleable. In mediation, communication takes place through what appears to be a blending of consciousness between the mediator and the spirit. In truth it is better described as communication by the use of resonance and mutual induction that results in the replication of pieces of each other's consciousness. One of the components of mediation is the highest form of clairsentience where there is no visible seam between sensing and knowing. Mediation is also the extension of what is done in mediumship and channeling. Like the medium, the mediator has sensitized the boundary between the preconscious and the conscious, but they take it several steps further so that each boundary between each layer of the aura and each level of consciousness is potentially a sounding board. Like the channeler, the mediator sends for a portion of themselves to seek a contact, but once they make the connection they adapt themselves to the conditions of that locus to steady the contact. Mediators communicate by becoming, which contains both the aspects of being and doing.

Some might confuse mediation with the experience of oneness of the mystics, but they are very different things indeed. The mediator deals primarily with information whereas the mystic's domain is essence. This information driven contact allows the mediator to simultaneously translate and relay while a mystic must meditate and work to convert essence into communication. The mystic is given more than the mediator but it is a lengthy process to truly understand what has been given. Another distinction is that mystics tend to eschew contact with anything that is not a direct messenger of Deity or a Deity themselves. Their true common denominator is that mediators and mystics both stand in the Middle Pillar and reach to Tiphareth.

Closing

In this chapter I have emphasized the distinctions between mediumship, channeling, and mediation to encourage their understanding through comparisons and contrasts. However, these practices arise from the same soil of psychism and magick. The characteristics of the flower or fruit they produce also depends upon the manner of their tending and the quality of the light of the soul of the practitioner. In the next chapter we'll examine some of the impediments to clear communication that impact on these as well as other forms of spirit contact.

Of Spirits: The Book Of Rowan

"Bee & Stars"

Impediments To Clear Spirit Contact

While many of the impediments to clear communication with spirits can be traced to problems with the practitioner or their technique, some are limitations inherent in the process of transmission. Other obstacles to clarity arise from human factors that are so much a part of daily life that they go unnoticed although their impact is profound. The difficulties presented in this chapter apply to virtually all forms of spirit contact.

The Metaphysics Of Spirit Contact

First let's examine the magickal mechanics of spirit contact— the nuts, the bolts, and the circuitry of the phenomenon. Spirit contact involves interactions and exchanges of energy, information and essence between different planes of reality. Spirit contact also passes through the levels of human consciousness, each with their attendant forms of processing. These interactions and exchanges are subject to laws. There are many different beliefs and theories as to what constitutes physical and metaphysical law, but the point to bear in mind is that spirit contact is not exempt, and that these practices do not have the equivalent of diplomatic immunity from the law. Spirit contact is subject to all the laws both physical and metaphysical pertinent to each plane of existence involved in the act of spirit contact. To make the most sense of spirit contact, and of communications derived from such contacts, the mechanism of the phenomenon must be understood for each plane of reality and each state of consciousness involved. A linear, flowchart-like, understanding of the mechanics of spirit contact could help to provide a frame of reference for the nonlinear qualities of the spirit contact experience. We are far from having such knowledge, but its attainment begins by recognizing that it is needed.

Many systems of esoteric thought recognize that there are veils, ring-pass-nots, the equivalent of quantum discontinuities, and the like, embedded within the spectrum of existence. In other words, there are real and identifiable boundaries between different states or planes of being. Sometimes these boundaries have their own reality, with their own qualities, and sometimes these boundaries are the artifacts of the interplay between the differences between one plane and another. Regardless of whether a boundary is real or an artifact, it has a tangible effect. An example of this is the refraction of light as it passes from air to water. If you hold a pencil in a glass of water, the image of the pencil is shifted by the difference in the way that water and air bend and transmit light, its refractive index. We know that the pencil has not been bent or broken though our eyes tell us otherwise. We know this because of our experience, not our senses. When a message from a spirit is refracted, deflected, by its passage through the planes we do not necessarily have the experience or the wisdom to compensate for that distortion. The distortion could change the time or timing or a host of other details and features in the message

These boundaries can act as filters, only allowing the passage of things with certain qualities, or as transformers, stepping voltage or frequency up or down. Most traditions that teach the doctrine of planes of being, planes of reality, also teach that as we rise on the planes the attributes of existence change as well. Close to the Earth plane, matter is dense, the overall vibration of things is low, time is highly linear, causality and form are paramount, etc. As you rise on the planes, matter becomes more ethereal, the overall vibration is higher, time becomes less linear, the sway of synchronicity and essence increase, etc. For communications to reach us they must work their way earthwards and in so doing must conform to the attributes of each plane they traverse. The energy, information, and essence of a spirit contact must be reshaped, normalized, and naturalized to a plane before it may pass to the next. When manifested in the plane of Earth and linear time, the action of the force of spirit is clothed, transformed and/or distorted by the unavoidable qualitative changes between the planes marked by these boundaries. This is not that different than the sorts of limitations that are laid onto a spirit as it passes through the steps to concretize an incarnation. These changes have the greatest impact on the essence component with a lesser impact on the energy and information.

In addition to the qualitative changes resulting from the passage from plane to plane, there are unavoidable degradations and losses in energy and information in spirit contact that result from a form of entropy. Think of this as spiritual friction or line loss. Some percentage, in particular of the energy and the information, is absorbed, dissipated, or misses the target. The ratio of noise to signal increases. Additionally, the metaphysical counterpart of static and atmospheric conditions affects the reception of the message. These atmospheric conditions are shaped, in the main, by astro-

Impediments To Clear Spirit Contact

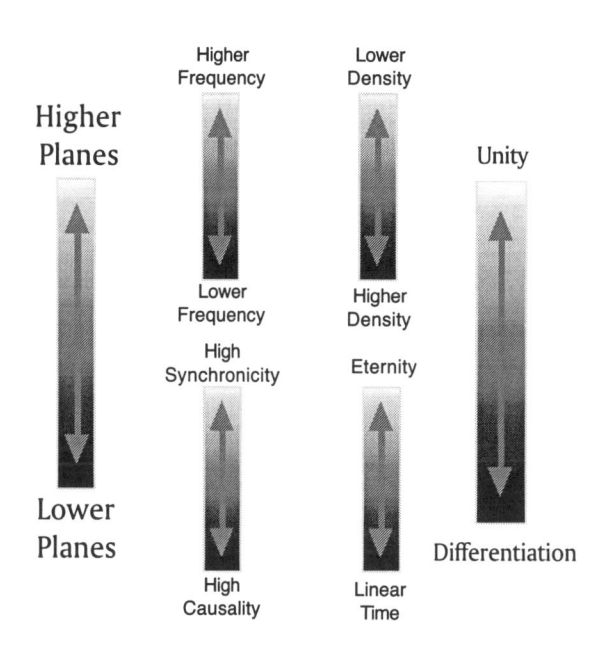

Higher Planes

Higher Frequency / Lower Frequency
Lower Density / Higher Density
High Synchronicity / High Causality
Unity / Differentiation
Eternity / Linear Time

Lower Planes

logical circumstances, shifts in the loci of populations of spirits, and other wide-ranging forces. These forms of interference generally do not affect the entirety of a message equally. Interference tends to be on specfic frequencies and as such will distort specific parts of a message rather than blocking it completely. In some ways it would be better if interference blocked a message completely. You have probably had the experience of listening to a radio in a car on a long trip; sooner or later, the signal of the radio station becomes overwhelmed by the static. Listeners will vary in their ability to listen past the static. It is important to note that if the song is familiar you will be able to identify it through a considerable amount of static. It is also true that you may imagine hearing a familiar song only to find that it is quite a different tune when the signal strengthens. The magnitude of the changes and losses derived from the metaphysics of transmission, however significant, pale in comparison to the alterations wrought by passage through the layers of the consciousness of the human receiving the message.

Levels, Probabilities, Perspectives

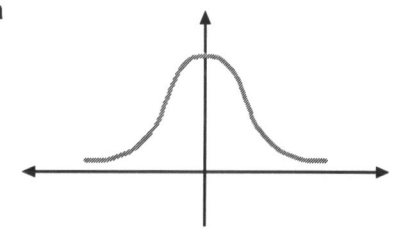

As was stated earlier, spirit contact is subject to the laws of each of the planes; the Hermetic Axiom of "as above so below", and the stricture of the Bell Shaped Curve are particularly relevant. The Hermetic Axiom suggests that we should look at the people in the world around us and apply what we see in them to discerning the motives, intelligence, and the wisdom of discarnate beings. This is more than just saying that discarnate entities can be brilliant, average, or moronic. There are refinements and changes in subtlety as one rises upwards from the physical plane, but the issues, concerns, order, disorder, health, illnesses, and challenges on the physical plane also have their corresponding equivalent on the other planes.

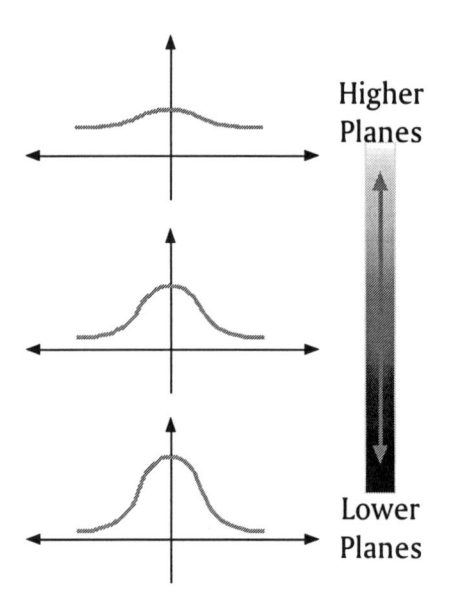

While the Hermetic Axiom speaks to the correlations and the connections between patterns and qualities, the Bell Shaped Curve, also known as gaussian distribution, speaks to numerical distributions and to probabilities. Virtually all naturally occurring characteristics and properties of groups, populations, or similar sets, when plotted, produce a curve similar to that shown in the figure. I believe that the quality and the clarity of spiritually conveyed information conforms to a bell shaped curve. I believe this also to be true for the intelligence and the wisdom of the sources of spiritually conveyed information. This is the law of averages; most of the distribution of any characteristic will be of average quality with smaller and smaller numbers as the extremes of high or low are approached. This pattern of probability may seem limiting or liberating depending upon your perspective. When a bird flies is it overcoming gravity or working with gravity? The quality of eyesight in the general population is on a bell shaped curve— until it is corrected by glasses. Not everything is correctable, but the curve is not fixed and unyielding even for those things that are not correctable. As a population grows in knowledge and wisdom the curve still applies, but it moves. The center of the curve today (the average, the median, the mode) will not be the center in the future. In the case of spirit contact and practitioners, before prescribing glasses, the type and the amount of correction needed must be uncovered. This is not easy because we are speaking of the mind's eye, an eye that is shaped by individual and collective factors.

Ignorance of the metaphysics of the planes may also impact on how information is interpreted. The probability curve flattens as we rise on the planes. This is a result of the tendency for unification as we rise on the planes which results from the summation of characteristics. The higher on the planes the source of the information, the greater the likelihood that it is from a being with greater knowledge and a wider perspective. Unfortunately, many times the practitioners lack the skill to determine the level that is the origin point for a communication. For those of you that are sticklers for strict magick theory, the probabilty curve ceases to have relevance when we rise to the discontinuity that is called the Abyss wherein Daath resides. This is rarely a consideration as there are almost no practitioners whose capabilities can reach that high.

Human Consciousness & Culture

In considering the human factor, some amount of these alterations, distortions, or losses may be attributed to the caliber of the individual practitioner's talent, and to their level of training or experience. It should also be pointed out, that if indeed the practitioner is in contact with a discarnate entity, that the clarity and intelligibility of the message is also determined by the talent and technique of the entity. For psychological and sociological reasons, there is a temptation to believe that the bulk of the problems with spirit contact are explainable as a question of prowess or training. It would be a mistake to stop investigating the underlying nature of spirit contact because many of its limitations can be assigned to matters of ability and skill or intent. There are patterns to the manifestation of spirit contact revealed by the intersection of magickal and the psychosocial models and laws that merit deeper investigation.

Different eras, cultures, and individual personalities have coped with the stress, tension, and the power of contact with higher consciousness through the roles and patterns of social behavior available to them. It is true that there is the potential for joy, enlightenment, and growth through higher (generally more inclusive) states of being, but it is equally true that there is potential for pain, delusion, and calamity. When spirit contact is not grounded into the social matrix of a person's life, like ungrounded magickal energy, it tends to dissipate or to leave unbalanced effects. Most current practitioners are the children of non-magickal societies that are disrespectful and disapproving of inner work. As such, they are heir to the psychological legacy of social and cultural environments that are impoverished in matters of active spiritual pursuits. Spirit contact takes a person outside of their normal boundaries. When the experience is over, those boundaries or new boundaries must be reestablished. The shape and the flexibility of those boundaries will decide how much of the communication is retained, and how much is clear or colored. Those boundaries, those contexts that would frame the experience are provided in part by the culture of the practitioner.

Traditional cultures that were more immanence-based, and closer in their relationship to the natural world, usually saw the individual that exhibited a gift for psychic expression as a resource to be incorporated into the fabric of society. The result of this perspective was the existence of roles, specific language, symbols, and metaphors, to allow for the useful expression of these gifts as a living part of a culture. The culture provided a set of structures that were designed to incorporate spiritually conveyed information into daily life and identity. Although I am focusing on the psychological and sociological impacts of culture on spirit contact, you should not forget that any structures that are a part of the life of a community also have an energetic expression. The thoughtforms maintained by the group mind of a culture are also part of the system that processes spirit contact. The existence of social and energetic patterns to ground psychic expression is no guarantee that the culturally sanctioned roles or symbols will provide for a healthy or a coherent translation of higher knowledge into the terms of the here and now. The only guarantee is that a larger number of communications will be received, contemplated, perhaps understood, and implemented. The social standing and psychological stability of a person acting within these roles varies in accordance with the nature of the culture.

These social constructs, that are scarce in modern Western culture, provide crucial grounding and insulation for those that are struck by the lightning flash of spirit contact. Without these social constructs, often the flash does little more than to reveal what already exists in the person and their culture rather than to illumine and to instruct. Indeed most of the spiritually conveyed information available in tapes, magazines, and lectures resembles popular science fiction wherein today's (often yesterday's) issues and concerns are clothed in tomorrow's fashions. A quick survey of the occult/ spiritualmetaphysical shelves of many bookstores will reveal a myriad of mutually incompatible worldviews spiritually conveyed from wise discarnate beings.

Personalities

The lightning flash also reveals the psychology of the culture of the practitioner. The problem of fear of intimacy and vulnerability, so prevalent in our society, impacts upon the modes used by conduits of knowledge from higher planes. There is fear in the opening of oneself to the presence of an-

Impediments To Clear Spirit Contact

other within the self. spirit contact, as it is generally understood and depicted, is as deeply intimate and as personal as sexuality. If it is contact with another being, then it is penetration, enclosure, and interpenetration. If it is contact with another part of the practitioner's self, the information may be devalued by the practitioner because of issues of self-esteem or self-confidence. If the contact is with the Akashic Record, or is clairsentience, or again is another part of the practitioner's self, many people will underrate the clarity or utility of the information precisely because it isn't presented as information from a discarnate being. There is psychological and social pressure for practitioners to perceive what they do as contact with specific entities. Given that, the practitioner must create a personality to define the shape of their contact. In the case of the practitioner who is actually in contact with a discarnate being, it should be considered that the personality of the being may still be more an artifact of the practitioner than of the being. This created personality provides the needed insulation from a reality that could be judged as indiscriminate contact with a wide range of sources of information of varying natures and veracities. The need for insulation and safety is paramount over other considerations in the creation of boundaries.

The majority of people engaged in spirit contact as a serious activity offer themselves as links or as spokespeople for one or perhaps a handful of entities. In fact it is the entity (and it's personality) that is the focus of the New Age community's response more so than it is the spiritually conveyed information or the practitioner. This is very problematic in a society prone to the cult of personality and to flight from freedom and its incumbent responsibility. My observations have led me to the belief that, nearly without exception, practitioners are not spokespeople for consistently specific entities. I and others who are psychically aware do definitely report changes in the auras of people engaged in spirit contact, as well as more palpable changes in their voice, or expression, or carriage, that could support their claims. However, correlation is not causation and the same changes could be the outcomes of contact with their higher selves, the human collective consciousness, the Akashic Record, the telesmatic images of culturally created thought and deity forms, or a variety of types of discarnate beings. This is in no way meant to imply a lack of sincerity on the part of practitioners or of a lack of utility for the information received. It does imply that cultural and psychological biases and weaknesses internalized by practitioners interfere significantly with clear reception, interpretation, and understanding. These biases and weaknesses express themselves through the individuals, and through the personalities that they create to articulate their experience of spirit contact.

One way to limit the impact of the frailties of the individual practitioner is to use personalities and protocols that are not created by the individual. The use of deity forms as a starting point may be a safer and clearer way to effective spirit contact. Traditional peoples and Neo-Pagans reduce the impact of the individual practitioner's quirks by using deity forms that are constructed collectively. Deity forms are the masks of the goddesses and the gods. Like masks, these forms are in part determined by the artistic sensibilities and the needs of the culture that creates them, and in part by the essence and pattern of the deity or intelligence that the mask must fit. Deity forms do change over time, but they tend to do so in a slow evolutionary fashion rather than in a radical or revolutionary way. Rapid change can happen when the environment changes rapidly, but even then it is more often a change in the mythology, the pattern of relationship between the forms, than in the essential nature of the forms. It can be argued that collective mythology starts as personal mythology. This may be true, but the kernel of truth in personal mythology is tended, trained, and pruned by many hands as it grows and transforms into collective mythology. practitioners could view their work as the creation of personal mythology that may be the seeds for future collective myths. Unfortunately, personal mythology is undervalued in our culture so the created personality of the spiritually conveyed entity is more comfortably treated as literal rather than metaphoric truth.

Literalism

The dominant Western religious and secular construct of paradigms (our current worldset) does provide roles and deity forms for spirit contact and other modes of psychic expression, but they are rooted in the spirit/matter dichotomy with its attendant problems. At this time, we who live in the sphere of influence of the Judeo-Christian-Islamic worldset are encouraged to see a dichotomy between spirit and matter. Spirit is also presented as being transcendent over matter. This splitting and ranking encourage, but do not require, the belief that spirit has the capacity to express itself in the physical realm in a way that ignores the limits of the physical universe and of the human psyche. This belief is the seed of literalism and fundamentalism that has grown and flourished in the age of Pisces. This belief that spirit can act supernaturally, unlimited by the laws of the physical, even affects people choosing paths other than the dominant Judeo-Christian-Islamic worldset, and can cause unnecessary, often unnoticed, distortion.

Impediments To Clear Spirit Contact

Joseph Campbell states, "For some reason which I have not yet found anywhere explained, the popular, unenlightened practice of prosaic reification of metaphoric imagery has been the fundamental method of the most influential exegetes of the whole Judeo-Christian-Islamic mythic complex.... In short, the social, as opposed to the mystical function of a mythology, is not to open the mind, but to enclose it: to bind a local people together in mutual support by offering images that awaken the heart to recognitions of commonality without allowing these to escape the monadic compound." [1] In our current setting this means that more often than not, the practitioner and the information conveyed, despite its spiritual focus, will be seen in literal rather than metaphoric terms. When seen as literal truth, what should be a source of unity and wisdom becomes a source of division, establishing camps and cliques of belief. Practitioners, as children of the Judeo-Christian-Islamic mythic complex, speak more often with the fundamentalism of a prophet than with the mythopoeic truth of a bard. This is potentially quite dangerous.

It is possible, within certain bounds, to gain awareness and control of the psychological constraints of socialization and of the psychic patterns of the worldset of our cultures of origin. Self-knowledge is the key to increasing clarity of reception, translation, and interpretation. This is not news to seekers on most paths. There is more to the self than the spirit or the soul— conscious understanding of the web of factors that make up the social and environmental context of the individual is central to self-knowledge.

In the present psycho-spiritual turbulence, normal for the cusp between two ages, there has been a sharp increase in the number of people attempting spirit contact. It is the nature of this cusp that there be a proliferation of the number of modes used to make these attempts. This proliferation produces chimeral hybrids of waning Pisces and waxing Aquarius, many beautiful but sterile, that are now being tested by our times. In seeking the new forms for the coming Aeon, we must be wary of not only the shortcomings of our current age but also those of the day we live in as well . It is my contention that spirit contact should be seen as a mythic activity in order to circumvent the worst of our current shortcomings. This insight is not an answer in itself because our sense of the mythic has become for the most part reduced to: myth as lies, myth as simplistic science, and myth as historical truth wrapped in the quaintness of legend.

To be fair, part of this propensity for the concretization of the energy of spirit into the forms of matter is in the essence of myth. According to Mircea Eliade, "The myth defines itself by its own mode of being... A myth always narrates something as having really happened, as an event that took place, in the plain sense of the term— whether it deals with the creation of the World, or of the most insignificant animal or vegetable species or of an institution." [2] In order to be understood by our normal waking consciousness myth must be told in a linear way. The error of the age is in forgetting that myth is metaphorical rather than historical, which is to say not valid as actual events. In other words, whatever happened in Atlantis, the Pleiades, ancient Central America, etc. are only true and useful if seen as metaphors and models existing outside of linear time.

Closing Thoughts

The phenomena of spirit contact is widespread, powerful, and is affecting ever increasing numbers of people on diverse spiritual paths. The literalism that has plagued spirit contact has often led to conflicts, disappointments, and disillusionments that do not promote growth. This can be changed. Even with these flaws, there is much in spirit contact that is useful because wisdom does find ways to manifest in virtually any format and venue. Despite all the difficulties inherent in the process, spirit contact has been the source or the inspiration for virtually all of the world's great teachings. This new child of the Old Age must be assessed with eyes open to the flaws that permeate our culture, flaws often as invisible as the waters are to fish. I believe that it is time to redefine spirit contact so that it may become primarily numinous myth rather than primarily myth of social expedience and local values. Spirit contact must be seen as magic, as social construct, and as myth. The forms and techniques that are being brought into manifestation now hold promise but like all other chimeral children of the flux between two Ages these forms and techniques require the refinement that only generations of use can create. Until then, we must strive to remain aware of the limits of what we have, who we are, and what we can become.

[1] Joseph Campbell, *The Inner Reaches Of Outer Space*, Harper & Row, 986
[2] Mircea Eliade, *Myths, Dreams, & Mysteries*, 960

Ghosts & Ancestors

When I first started writing this book and I would describe its theme to my friends, I found an interesting divergence in their assumptions about the topics that I would cover. Some assumed that the book would be mostly about ghosts. Others thought that the book would cover spirit guides, God/dess/es, and the like. Only a very small minority concluded that the spirits of the departed, and the Great Ones, etc., could comfortably share space between the covers of one book. As you read this chapter consider how it relates to all that you know about discarnate beings and everything covered in this book. It is particularly important that you read this chapter closely in order to understand the chapter "Spiritual Lineage" which expands upon the ideas covered under the categories of ghosts and ancestors.

I will not be sharing specific techniques for spirit contact here as there are many sources for such material, instead I focus on the nature of ghosts and ancestors. If you know what is occurring beneath the level of outward phenomena and the procedural steps of techniques, you can fathom them more easily. Although there are the relationships between that which we call the ancestors and that which we call ghosts and hauntings, there are very important distinctions that must be understood in order to work with any of these in a safe and productive manner. We will begin with ghosts and spirits of the human dead and then explore what is meant by the ancestors.

Dying

To properly understand ghosts and human spirits of the dead it is necessary to understand the process of dying as well as the qualities of time of the linear and nonlinear types.

Being born is not just the birth itself but is also the pregnancy, the conception, and the choices that were made that led to that new life. The process of dying is much like the process of coming into an incarnation only reversed. Death is the final harvest and the preservation of a life's work. In death we shed the various bodies that are the vehicles used by a spirit in an incarnation. To elucidate the concept of death as a harvest consider agricultural images. We cut the plant from its roots and we separate the grain from the chaff. We pick the grapes and through the alchemy of fermentation create the wine that will last for years beyond the harvest. Each harvest, the most promising seeds are set aside to be planted in the next year. There are limits to all metaphors, comparisons and similes but these clarify more than they obscure. There are many systems for counting and naming the subtle bodies, and I am not endorsing one system over another as they are often equal parts of truth and doctrine. In this description I will adhere to what I believe is the essence of the process.

First, the physical body is shed and those experiences, the learning of that life, that are stored in the flesh are translated into energetic patterns that rise into the Etheric body, which is the subtle body that is closest to the physical. This is the layer of the aura that clings closely to the body. What the body has learned is stored at the cellular level and in the learned reflexes that are stored in the nervous system. There is a long standing description/perception by those with the *sight* that there is a silver cord that connects the subtle bodies to the physical body. During dying, it is severed when what the body has learned has been fully transferred to the subtle bodies. This is the silver cord that is seen by some during astral travel and is an analogue of the umbilical cord. When we were in our mother's womb, we were connected to her via the umbilical cord to the placenta that rooted within her. Once born, our physical body was like a placenta that drew nourishment from the Earth Mother which in turn both anchored and fed our subtle bodies. Like the placenta, the physical body disconnects from the Earth Mother so that we may move on. The silver cord also has actual and symbolic resonances to the 32nd path in the Qabala that connects the sphere of the Earth and the sphere of the Moon. The passage through the birth canal and the passage through the tunnel oft reported by those with near death experiences is in essence one and the same. At this point in the process the ghost most resembles the incarnation that has just ended both in appearance and in personality. Here the grain is cut then separated from the chaff.

What follows next is the delicate and intricate process of the translation and the transfer of what the personality and the soul have learned during their sojourn on Earth into progressively more rarefied subtle bodies. One way to conceptualize this is the conversion of a large quantity of data into an abstract or an elegant set of theories or principles. Another apt comparison would be the deep insights that hopefully come at the completion of an important sequence of life experiences expressed as a poem or a painting. The juice, the essence, of what is contained in each layer of the aura is extracted and collected in the layer above it. The subtle bodies that are emptied of their essence are then shed, like the physical body, and are deposited onto the plane of being to which they correspond. Even though they are empty husks, they persist for some time until they lose their cohesion and disintegrate. If the ghost is encountered during this phase of the dying process it still bears some resemblances to the person that died, but less so as the process continues. The person examines the whole of their life and transforms it into a mythic saga which describes their journey on Earth with greater depth. It should be remembered that mythic truth is not journalism nor is a portrait a photograph. Like grapes in the process of becoming wine, the individual grapes can no longer be tasted when they are juice. Then as time goes on, the juice no longer tastes like grape juice. The flavor changes to become a summation of the soil, the climate, and all the factors and the choices made that led to that specific vintage.

The final process is one in which the personality is distilled into the individuality. The individuality is also the highest self and is the part of the person that is truly eternal. At this point there are no more subtle bodies to be shed, rather it is about integrating the old linear life with the evolving spirit of the individual. At this stage, the resemblance to the incarnation that has just finished is very slight. It is like looking at the photograph of a child and the photograph of an elderly person. If you know that they are the same person you can see the similarities. If you do not know, then it is just as likely that you will not see them as the same individual. At this point everything that could be resolved has been resolved and brought into focus. What remains is that which is carried by the eternal self, the individuality, and the seeds of future incarnations. These seeds contain both the progress that has been made and also those areas that need additional work. The incarnation is truly finished at this point, the person is truly dead. Yet, they are also profoundly vital and striving, with guidance, to choose the proper times, places, and characteristics for future incarnations. The seeds that will be planted are now set aside and prepared.

There are other ways of summarizing this process. One would be to see it as the sequence of the Four Elements folding into each other as we rise on the planes of being. The essence of Earth, the body, rises into Air. This rarefied essence condenses in the Air into clouds of Water. The celestial Water releases the bolt of Fiery Lightning that unites the beginning and the end. This description of the dying can also be seen as the Nephesch, nesting into the Ruach, which in turn nests into the Neschamah. Another yet would be to see it in terms of the modalities with the Mutable becoming the Fixed modality, and then the Cardinal modality as the last stage of dying. This progression also follows the pattern of the predominance of energy giving way to the predominance of information, and finally essence as you rise on the planes. I will not elaborate these summaries any further but suggest that you meditate upon each sequence a number of times. Each time you do so, new meanings and nuances should emerge. If no new insights emerge, do some research, dig deeper, and meditate again.

The length of linear time that is needed to complete the process of dying, varies dramatically from person to person. The nature of the death determines a portion of this as does the nature of the person dying. Tragic circumstances or dying in an unusual state of consciousness (such as a drug overdose) can slow the process. This delay in the process can stem from the physical body's memory not having adequate time to transfer itself into the Etheric body. Another complicating factor is that most people need some amount of time to prepare themselves emotionally for death and the energy of these unprocessed emotions can clog the channel. It is well known that leaving unfinished tasks can slow the process, but in my experience this only has a significant impact when the unfinished tasks relate directly to the purposes of that incarnation, not just to the desires of the personality that is dying. If someone presses the question for an approximate duration, my usual response is somewhere in the neighborhood of 35 to 49 days to complete the first phase.

I base this duration on my observations of spirits of the recently departed and upon certain correspondences to the influences of the Moon, the Sun, and the Stars. Thirty five days is enough time for one complete lunar cycle with the buffer of a week for the process to begin and end. The lunar cycle has an especially strong impact on the lower subtle bodies. There are also powerful tides moved by the solar cycle of the solstices, equinoxes, and cross-quarter days. The interval of time between each of the eight holidays in the Wheel of the Year is roughly 45 days. For some, the change in the solar tides equivalent to one turn of stations on the Wheel is enough to push the first phase to completion. The number 49 is symbolic of a reconciliation between linear time and non-linear time as it is the equivalent of a week of weeks. The seven days of a week corresponds to the Seven Elder Planets. When 7 weeks have passed, a complete cycle of the Elder Planets is completed. There is also a correspondence to Tibetan Buddhism wherein the 49 days after a death is known as the Bardo period during which the life just completed is assessed and confronted through a series of visions. The length of time needed to complete the second and third phases is too idiosyncratic to offer any guesses. Moreover, these phases occur at higher planes of being where time as we know it has little meaning.

You may wish to go over these paragraphs again as the process of dying explains many of the mechanisms for the phenomenon that are described in the remainder of this chapter.

Ghosts & Hauntings

What are commonly called ghosts or hauntings actually covers a broad range of possibilities and phenomena. If you are to have useful and healthy contacts with ghosts, it is necessary to understand their nature and to be able to identify their type. Much of the literature on ghosts tends to categorize them by the forms of their manifestations or by the themes they portray. This may be productive if your aim is the study of folklore but it is less useful for an occultist. It is useful to examine accounts of ghosts and hauntings, but with a critical eye focused on the metaphysical content rather than the content that appeals to human sentiment. The following paragraphs express how I classify ghosts according to their composition and their essence. For the sake of simplicity I will categorize them as *recordings*, *shells*, *spirits of the dead*, and *living ghosts*.

Recordings

The simplest and most frequently encountered type of ghost or haunting is no more than a recording that replays itself when the conditions are right. In these cases there is no spirit present, no soul trapped between the worlds, nor any other romantic misconception. What is present is the artifact of a life. This recording may be perceived by any combination of one or more of the senses. It may be also be experienced as a particular atmosphere or blend of emotional tones that do not correspond to specific physical senses. Depending upon the force of the recording, it may only be apparent to sensitives or it may be clear to even those that are usually headblind. It may be quite blurry and muddled or crystal clear. A recording may be very brief like a song skipping while you listen to a stereo or a lengthier recording like a loop of video playing on a museum kiosk. If it is a longer recording the order, sequence, and the duration of those things that are conveyed will probably have some distortions and some transpositions.

Of Spirits: The Book Of Rowan

Although there are several means by which such recordings can be impressed upon a location or an object, they all require a powerful burst of energy and material that is capable of holding a patterned charge. Usually the source of energy is an exceptionally powerful emotional outburst at the time of the recording. Often a tragic or violent circumstance is the surest source for a blast of sharply defined energy. On occasion, joy, love or other transcendent emotions can flare in a way that records a blessed moment. If every strong flash of psychic energy had the capacity to impress an easily accessed recording onto the substance of the world, we would live in a world overflowing with hauntings. Since we do not, there must be other predicating factors. If we were to compare this process to photography, the burst of energy would be like a flash of light. The object or location of the haunting would be the equivalent of the photographic film. As we know, film varies in its sensitivity, speed, and the fineness of its grain. There must also be a lens and the attendant parts that allow the image to be focused upon the film.

Not all buildings, objects, or locations can act as film that records psychic energy. The capacity to hold patterned energy, psychic data, is determined by the properties of the materials present, their shape, and the geometry of the volumes they enclose or define. Buildings, objects, and locations also vary in the length of time that they will hold an impression until it fades away like a photograph left in the sun. The way that the film is *developed* and *printed* also has its part to play. External factors can greatly modify the quality and longevity of an impression and the amount of energy required to create an impression. Imagine a sandy river bank with a bird walking upon it. Its footprints are easily recorded by the wet sand and just as easily erased. If there is the right kind of disruption, such as a flood that changes the course of the river, those footprints may be filled with a fine clay that eventually becomes a fossil. Those footprints may then outlive our civilization. There are forces that flow like rivers beneath our feet in what amounts to the Earth's energetic circulatory system that we map as ley lines. There are also forces that radiate down upon us from the heavens that we name and measure with the astrology. These forces from above and forces from below affect the creation of hauntings, just as surely as a flood changing the course of a river can create a fossil.

Hauntings require an external energy source to be viewed just as a movie requires light to be projected. The character of the recording determines the type and the amount of energy needed to make it perceivable. Some apparitions are only visible when the moon is full or when the planets are in an alignment that echoes the conditions when the recording was made.

In the Northern countries there are tales of hauntings that only awaken when the aurora borealis glows which is powered by solar flares. Many hauntings that persist for centuries are located over places where the power that flows in the earth surges to the surface. These vortices of earth power can bubble with the slow steady constancy of hot springs or can periodically erupt like geysers. Another source of energy to activate a haunting is living human beings. Some hauntings demand only the presence of a certain number of humans or a particular powerful flow of energy from an individual. Others require that a person be present whose energy signature is in some way keyed to that of the recording. By examining the conditions surrounding periods of activity and dormancy, it is possible to discover the parameters that govern a particular haunting.

Traditionally, we think of hauntings as being associated with deaths, but if you think on the process there are a wide range of situations that will create a recording. This is especially true for objects or locations, such as jewelry or temples, used for religious or spiritual purposes since it is the nature of the activities connected with these to be associated with carefully shaped thoughts and emotions. In these cases the recordings are generally not of specific events, but rather are a summation of what has transpired. Secular objects or locations that are prominent in the public eye or have symbolic meaning can also be imbued
with power and memory. Examples of these include bridges, statues, monuments, and mountains that are connected to the identity of a city, a nation, or a people. Technically, it is better to say that these are cases of thought-forms anchored to physical objects, but the legends and folklore surrounding these things don't often make that distinction.

Shells

If a ghost or a haunting responds to contact with living humans with non repetitive actions that indicate real interaction, then more than just a recording remains. If a haunting follows a person to a new location this is also an indication that it is not just a recording. Make sure that you rule out the possibility of the relocation of an object or a piece of a building that was the anchor for the haunting. Sometimes the haunting can be contained in something as small as a piece of furniture, a door, or in some salvaged architectural elements such as moldings or stonework. Interactivity does not prove that a guiding intelligence or a soul is present. The clever responses and actions offered by a well designed video game, web site, or computer program certainly give the appearance of a guiding presence, but they are no more than an impression of their creators' thought processes.

As I covered in the description of dying, numerous subtle bodies are shed and discarded. Normally these empty shells wither and decay much as the physical body does. Without the nourishment provided by a living physical body, these lower subtle bodies lose their conformation and cohesion. These shells of subtle bodies also lose their linkage to one another as the focus of soul journeys up and out of them. These emptied husks break down into simpler and simpler patterns of energy until they are absorbed into the plane of being to which they are native. That is the normal order of things, but if vital energy is supplied the disintegration can be forestalled. In rarer circumstances, if a motive or guiding principle remains or is inserted, some linkages may remain between the discarded subtle bodies. Depending upon the degree of preservation and the amount of energy supporting these reanimated shells, a considerable amount of the departed person's knowledge and personality may be present.

These ghosts that are shells of the departed can display the full range of human behavior from the benefic to the depraved. They can be very like the individual that they were in life or they can be so distorted that they are a barely recognizable caricature. Consider that the shell does not have the tempering influence of the higher self. How would you behave if you did not have your soul? If the personality is balanced and well developed then there is a good chance that the behavior will be balanced as well. Also consider that there may have been decay in the shells before they were re-energized and it may also be that only two or three of the subtle bodies are still linked. These losses can result in behavior that resembles intoxication, mental illness or brain damage. It is also possible to have more than one shell derived from the same individual. These disassociated shells are the ghostly equivalent of multiple personalities. No negative judgments should be made about a deceased person's character based on a contact with their shell. We are more than the sum of our parts and the parts viewed without the benefit of context or the blessing of unity are not a fair semblance.

So what circumstances bring about the creation of a shell? All the lower subtle bodies persist for a time after death. If an effort is made to contact a recently departed person, it is possible to unintentionally contact a shell rather than their soul or spirit. The psychic energy poured into making the contact provides the current to awaken the shell. A good medium or psychic sensitive should be able to negotiate past the shell and make a proper connection but that is not always the case. A better question to ask is why do some shells persist? Human vital force is the form of energy that is most easily absorbed by shells as that is what sustained them in life. Other forms of energy may be substituted with varying degrees of success depending upon the nature of the shell and the qualities of energetic environment that the shell is inhabiting. In descending order of ease of absorption, vitality may be drawn from the life force of animals, the life force of plants, life force embedded in an object or a place, and lastly the elemental forces of nature.

It is fairly common to experience a drop in temperature in the presence of an active manifestation of a ghost. This is caused by the ghost pulling in energy to counteract the expenditure of energy used in its manifestation. Hauntings that are recordings do not cause a temperature drop so if this occurs it is either a shell or an actual spirit of the dead. It is valuable to determine if this drop in temperature is subjective or a physical reality. If cold is perceived but a thermometer does not record the change, then the energy is being drawn out of the people present rather than the environment. Knowing that the energy is being drawn from people gives some leverage in controlling a manifestation. If the energy is being drawn from the environment it is more likely to be a spirit of the dead or at the least an exceptionally well preserved shell.

Some shells are powered by the emotions of their remaining loved ones, especially if the grieving becomes an unhealthy protracted bereavement. The person or persons continue to call up the image of the departed in their minds and their emotional energy will flow to the shell. In an odd way this functions somewhat like distance healing with the energy working to restore the empty shell. This does not *trap* the soul or spirit of the departed. No matter how popular a plot element it has become in films and fiction, we do not have the power to do such a thing with just misdirected emotions. However, it can cause emotional discomfort to the evolving spirit that has moved on and sees the state of its loved ones. It must also be an annoyance to see a poor copy of yourself strutting about on the stage of the world using your name.

It is also possible for a shell to receive energy to persist from other sources. If the person who died was prominent in the minds of many people and/or their life story strongly resonated to some archetypal pattern, then their shell may be supported by a tie to this more diffuse but sizable source if energy. This can also occur in cultures with a strong belief in ghosts as a more generalized phenomenon. It is also possible for a shell to be conjured and maintained through ritual magick. Indeed much of what is called necromancy is actually the use and control of the shells of the departed. One bit of good news for the squeamish is that those pale forms knocking about at the behest of the necromancer are not spirits in the full sense of the word. If the need, desire, and circumstances are right, shells reanimated through these two means can persist for a very long time.

There are many cultures with stories about hungry ghosts with wrathful, lustful, or malicious intent. These are shells. If desires or primal needs survive in a shell it can drain energy from the living. I have seen more than one shell at a bar or pub taking advantage of the atmosphere and the reduced defenses of the patrons. The practices used to quell these disruptive spirits are often dismissed as superstition but they do have legitimate psychological and metaphysical functions. It is important to note that the conventional wisdom of traditional rites and customs do for the greater part work, but perhaps not for the reasons ascribed to them. This is also true for many current metaphysical beliefs as well. The modern custom of sending a *trapped* ghost into the light through spiritual and magickal effort does not free a spirit. A shell may report that it doesn't know it's dead or that it can't move on, but it is not an ensouled being. Sending it on its way does dissolve a shell back into the matrix of light that is the repository of the material from which life and consciousness are assembled. This is a good thing for those that are still living and for the spirit that has moved on.

When people die who have strong psychic abilities and/or have achieved high levels of initiation in magickal systems, there are special considerations to be pondered in the disposition of their shells. Devotion to a sport or to an active art such as dance changes the shape of the physical body and ingrains special reflexes into the nervous system. Repeated use over a lifetime of the esoteric skills and powers changes the shape of the lower subtle bodies and embeds within them the pattern of those practices. The shell of such a person retains many of the skills and powers that they garnered while living. If in life a person was proficient at sense, shaping, and moving energy, their shell has the potential to do the same. These special shells are more adept at collecting and keeping energy to remain coherent and active. This facility in remaining energized also extends to drawing power from the earth and sky in addition to living sources. A number of esoteric systems have as a part of their training the creation of a magickal personality, a working fetch, a co-walker or some other extension of the core personality. A well-developed secondary focus of consciousness, such as a magickal personality, can become the core of shed subtle bodies resulting in a particularly potent shell.

There is a long historical record that indicates that the ghosts of magickal people are different from the garden-variety ghost. They were different in life and remain so in death. A recurrent theme in many of these stories is that they can choose to haunt a place or accomplish a task as they die. If the force and the focus of the will remains strong as the person dies, their shed subtle bodies will endeavor to carry out those last intentions. In some regards these shells are more like spells housed in complex thought forms. Even when there is no intent to do so, the shells of magickal people do tend to last longer.

In some traditions the magickal tools of the dead, such as wands, swords, rings, etc., are either carefully passed on with appropriate rituals or laid to rest. It is important that the magickal tools of the dead be treated with due respect and care. Whatever choices are made, the potential outcomes and sequelae should be deliberated. In life, work is done to bind the tools to the practitioner's energy and to create lasting impressions within them. Those bonds are not broken by death and the shells remain connected to the tools. Sometimes when a magickal tool is passed on and continues to be used, the shell of its previous owner will be transformed and become a permanent part of that tool. If this transfiguration occurs, the shell is invested into the tool, where it refines over time in a manner similar to the distillation of essence in the latter stages of the dying process. The result is that what remains over time bears little resemblance to the personality of the original owner but does carry a polished portion of what they achieved in life. Many ancient and holy relics, sites, and artifacts evolved into what they are through this process.

Spirits Of The Dead

Some apparitions or contacts are actually the spirits of the dead. What I mean by that is that the soul and/or spirit of a departed person is the guiding intelligence behind the presence experienced. To my way of thinking, soul and spirit are not identical. You may use different words or concepts, but to make the next point requires a distinction between these subtle parts of self. When we are born a part of us journeys into dense matter and into linear time. Another part of us remains outside of the frame of time in what I often call eternity. The soul is the spiritual presence anchored to the body and to linear time that grows and learns over the course of a lifetime. The spirit remains outside of linear time and for many is known as the Higher Self or the Divine Spark. That which the soul has gathered in its journey is deposited in the spirit with the completion of the dying process. The soul joins with the spirit like water poured from a river in to a bay. All the lives that a person has lived are summed up in the spirit.

Unlike recordings or shells, spirits of the dead have continued to evolve. It is possible for a recording or a shell to grow, to add on, but not to evolve. This means that the person contacted may be different than they were in life because evolution is change. If they are in the middle to late part of the dying process, they may still have many of the emotions and aspirations of the life they just completed. Their soul has not completely mingled with their spirit just as the temperature and the salinity of a river can extend some distance into a bay. Nonetheless, they will not respond exactly as they would have in life. They will have gained new perspectives on their life because they are viewing it from several distances and several vantage points. If they are contacted when they have completed the process of dying, they will be very different indeed. Let me give an example from life that illustrates this change. I have clear recollections of my teenage years and of my high school friends, but I am who I am today. If I run into one of those friends that I have not seen in decades, I will know them and yet I will not *know* them. I will have feelings for them but in most cases it will feel as if it were another life. Imagine the changes wrought by the separation of death rather than decades, the memories of many lives, and the perspective of seeing linear time from the outside. Another glimpse at the changes brought about by death can be seen in the accounts of people who have had a near death experience. The vast majority of people with near death experiences have dramatically changed personalities and outlooks on life. I am emphasizing these changes because, I have seen people disbelieve a genuine contact or be discomforted by one because their departed loved ones did not behave in a way that matched their recollections and expectations. This is more common when it is the living that initiates the contact with the discarnate person. Sometimes the spirit does not see the point to the contact or has a very different agenda for what should be discussed. Generally if the spirit is initiating the contact, they have something to communicate that matches the needs and wants of the living.

Despite the changes that come about through the work and the evolution that continues after we leave the physical plane, love still matters. Aside from the bonds of karma, The bond of love is more durable than any other. But remember that all things change and though love survives death, it will be a different kind of love than that which existed in life. If you believe in reincarnation, as I do, consider how many loves you must have had over time and how feeling that truth would change your perspective. If the spirit has been dead for many years, it is still possible for them to assume the form and the personality that they once had. Just as we carefully choose the right words to say or the right things to wear for important occasions, spirits will carefully choose the manner of their manifestation. As much is communicated by how they appear as by what they say.

Living Ghosts

It may seem a contradiction in terms, but a living person may be experienced as ghost. This state of affairs can be a little confusing to all involved, especially to the ghost who is being assured that they are dead. There are a number of circumstances that can create this situation. The easiest to grasp is that of a very dense astral projection. When out of body travel occurs it generally is not witnessed except by those with first-rate second sight. When the traveler can be perceived by others, it is because a larger portion of their subtle bodies have followed the focus of consciousness far from the body. Although a confluence of external factors can make this happen with any astral projection, it is more likely to occur as the result of extended work at perfecting astral projection or during a near death experience or a deep coma. One of the names for this type of phenomena is the doppelganger which is German for "double walker" which is an apt description for what is actually occurring. As you might imagine this requires a fair amount of energy which explains the need for keeping a person engaged in astral projection bundled up and warm. The chill that they often experience is not that different from the cooling effect of ghosts draining energy, except in this case it is supporting the extension of their own subtle bodies.

The experience of a living ghost or apparition may be the result of psychic time travel. Every night when we sleep we journey, our spirit travels. We do not remember all these voyages any more than we remember all our dreams, but this does not make them any less real. If an effort is made to contact a spirit through ritual or psychic means and no contact is made in the present, sometimes the call and the search will broadcast back in time. It is then possible to contact the dreaming self before the time of their death in linear time. It is less common, but a person traveling in their dreams may move forwards to a time past their death and appear unbidden to those with whom they have a connection. All these forms of communication are the natural outgrowth of the clairvoyance, clairaudience, and clairsentience. Humans are all gifted with at least these three *clairs* whether or nor they are aware of the gifts during waking consciousness. There is one other type of living ghost to consider if the person being contacted has been dead for a long time. It is possible that the supposedly dead person has reincarnated, in which case they can act as a relay linking to their spirit outside of time that holds all that they have been. For this to occur, the reincarnated person must be sleeping or in some other special state of consciousness.

The surest way to determine if the ghost is actually a living being is to look for the silver cord that reaches back to their body. The silver cord is actually the analog of the central column of energy that flows around and through the spine. The cord is that which links the subtle bodies together acting much like the umbilical cord, the spinal cord and the corpus collosum. The silver cord may not appear as silver to you. You may also perceive it as a woven braid of energies or as a strand of gemstones or as any number of forms or colors. Even if the spirit is a living human, you may not see the cord at first. Although it is firmly entrenched in the literature, few people have actually seen it. It is in the nature of psychic perception that attention creates detail; often things are not visible until they are sought.

The Ancestors

There is a long history for the reverence of the ancestors. Indeed some of the earliest archaeological evidence for humans expressing their spiritual drive is in funerary practices and in the honoring of the ancestors. Whether it is in the ancient past or in current non-monotheistic cultures, many anthropologists and sociologists will commonly call these practices *ancestor worship*. This is an unfortunate choice of words, because the people that venerate their ancestors know that their ancestors are not Goddesses or Gods. Belief in the power of the ancestors is normally associated with a worldview that populates the universe with a complicated ecology of spiritual beings and spiritual forces. Each type of spirit has its place and merits respect and treatment appropriate to its niche. It is not surprising that interest in working with the ancestors is on the rise in the Neo-Pagan community as it is an almost inevitable descendant of this worldview.

Henceforth in this chapter, Ancestors with an uppercase "A" will refer to the Mighty Dead and a lowercase "a" will refer to biological forerunners and their spirits. The Ancestors can be called upon for assistance with the same type of expectation that they will respond that is held for prayers to higher beings; this is not generally true for ghosts. This separation of the two is not meant as a slight or a judgment, but as a recognition that they are categorically different. Merely dying does not make you one of the Ancestors. In most traditional cultures throughout the world, only those people who have led exceptional lives become available as sources for guidance and information after they have died. People who become the Ancestors do not fade from memory because their stories are told and retold. In the telling, their stories are embroidered upon and become local legends. By the way, exceptional means that they are exemplary which can mean good, bad, and everything in between. A really bad Ancestor makes for a really good cautionary tale.

The first source for kinship that most people associate with the Ancestors is that of a blood relationship. There is indeed is a powerful connection produced by direct lineal descent to an Ancestor but there is nearly as strong a tie for less direct connections that come from sharing the blood of a tribe, ethnicity, or similar grouping. Sharing similar genetic patterns to those that the Ancestors had in life creates receptors in the subtle bodies that are pre-tuned to the type and the frequency of signals of the Ancestors. This is an autonomic process; without thought or effort, the physical genetic patterns are echoed by similar structures in the lower subtle bodies. It is comparable to having preset favorite stations on a radio; if a button is pressed, it jumps to that station. Like calls to like and through resonance and induction the physical body and the lower subtle bodies receive the energetic patterns that consciousness perceives as messages from the Ancestors. It is important to note that these keying patterns are not in the higher subtle bodies. Like the personality, ethnicity and race are localized in the time and space of a lifetime, whereas the higher subtle bodies operate at the more abstracted level of humanity as a whole and of connection to the Divine.

This does not mean that only people from a small and tightly focused gene pool have a strong connection to the Ancestors. It may be generally true that a high proportion of ancestry from one ethnicity is an advantage in connecting with the Ancestors of that ethnicity, but human genetics is a complicated subject that science is just beginning to explore. It may be that in the myriad throws of the genetic dice required to create one individual, that the right sequence, the right keying phrase, maybe granted to one who has but a drop of a line's blood. Although exceedingly rare, there are individuals without a drop of ethnicity's blood who nonetheless resonates to a seemingly foreign heritage. Nature repeats itself, sometimes with purpose and some times not. An example from medicine that demonstrates this is the occasional but repeatable matching of bone marrow for transplantation between individuals from stock as far apart as the globe allows. It is also possible for someone who is as fully of one blood as is possible in modern times to have lost the throw of the dice that grants the keying sequence. This does not mean that they are bereft of means to connect with the Ancestors of their biological cultures of origin.

The functional component is the energetic pattern in the lower subtle bodies which acts as the wave guide, the interface, for connecting to the Ancestors. The subtle bodies are more plastic, more alterable, than the physical body. The needed pattern can be grafted onto the subtle bodies. If all goes well, the pattern becomes a seamless part of the overall energy and form of that person that persists over time. It is the longevity of this pattern that marks it as different from the chameleon-like changes in the aura employed by mediums and psychic sensitives to realize similar contacts. There are three methods by which this grafting can be accomplished with consistent results: by adoption, by affinity, and by initiation. In actuality, these methods often overlap and combine, but for the sake of clarity I will present them separately.

Adoption

In this context adoption is not a matter of legalities or of an official approval, rather it is a question put before the court of the heart. Adoption within this sphere of activity can therefore include the heart connections of siblinghood and marriage in addition to those of parental acknowledgment. Most cultures, currently or in their history, have ceremonies and rituals to make a person a member of a family, a clan, or a tribe. These ceremonies and rituals generally contain a visible, often public, sequence of symbolic actions that provide the starting point for a process that continues in the invisible realms. An orphan kitten or puppy that is washed then rubbed with the scent of the adoptive mother's milk or the scent of its future siblings will often be accepted. In essence this process is not that different. The surface of the individual's aura is marked with a part of the keying sequence. If the individual's heart and the hearts of those that would adopt them nourish this freshly seeded pattern with positive emotions, it will persist and grow. If this flow of love continues long enough, the keying pattern will sink in and will root itself in the lower subtle bodies. As their new life as a member of the family, clan, or tribe becomes more established and relationships deepen, they become present in that particular group mind and/or group soul. Sometime after this occurs, they will be touched by the Ancestors because they have become visible to them in the interplay that weaves the life of the community. It is the touch of the Ancestors that makes the graft permanent by completing the circle that joins the past and the future in the now. As with any process, success is not always assured;

nonetheless adoption is the most reliable but often the slowest of these methods.

Affinity

Strong emotions and sharply focused mental activity creates patterns within our subtle bodies. Those gifted with psychic talents can create specific patterns at will, but even those without special gifts can do the same though it may take longer. The power of the zeal of a convert, a connoisseur, or a devotee should not be underestimated. People can and do fall in love with cultures that are distant from their ancestry. Sometimes this comes from a person finding their sensibilities, aesthetics, and disposition better expressed in another culture. Sometimes a longing from a past life is awakened by what is foreign but familiar. Often it is a combination of influences that leads them to love the ethos of a people. This love and passion often pushes them to become as knowledgeable or more knowledgeable about the traditions of a culture than those born to it. As they are steeped in the lore, its colors, flavors, and textures begin to permeate their being. For some individuals this leads to a deep and abiding desire to become one with the subject of their studies. Over time, their natural affinity, their studies, and their admiration of the culture create a persistent pattern in their energy that approximates the mark of that people. If this is acceptable to the Ancestors, they will make a contact and begin to subtlety insinuate the changes needed to correct the keying pattern. When and where it is possible, those that have strived so diligently will often be approached by members of the culture that they admire. Inclusion within the social mind of the people then begins to refine the connection to the Ancestors in much the way that occurs in adoptions.

Wanting something is not the same as having an affinity for it. I have met many people that make the mistake of confusing the two and remain perpetual wannabees. If it can not be found within, it will never be found without. If the desire to become a part of a culture or a people is expressed in terms of what it means or represents, it is a warning that perhaps a true affinity is not present. If the desire to become a part of a culture or a people is an escape rather than a homecoming, it is unequivocally not an affinity. If you wish to test the potential of desire that has been called an affinity, apply the rules of love. Think on what you know of infatuation, of being in love with love, of the depth of soul love, of the repetition of that which is a person's *type*, and of the sweet hardships of mature love. Then examine the nature of the desire and the calling to join with that culture. Gaining the acceptance of the Ancestors through affinity is a quest that few are suited for and even fewer can complete. When this quest can be attained the reward truly is a treasure.

Initiation

When a family, a clan, a tribe, or a people have overtly magcikal rituals to cement the connection to the Ancestors, then the route of initiation is a possibility. Through the use of the sacred sciences of that people, the energetic pattern keyed to the Ancestors is implanted into the aura of the candidate. This may be one ritual or may be a series over a period of time to make sure that the graft takes. This method of connecting with the Ancestors tends to be reliable but is limited to those that meet the criteria of the initiators. Beyond the judgment of the person's character, there are normally requirements for some type of esoteric talent or some sign that indicates that the candidate is appropriate. The culture will determine the particulars of the initiation. Is it entry into a medicine society or clan? Does it mark the making of some form of clergy? What obligations and duties attend the privilege of admittance into such a select company? On the surface this may be the most direct portal for outsiders to connect with the Ancestors of a people, but the route to the portal has many twists and turns. The connection to the Ancestors granted by an initiatory process generally contains connections to other entities as well. Cultures that use the sacred sciences in an overt manner tend also to have highly developed linkages to the patrons of their people and to their Great Ones. Moreover, most magickal groups that give initiations also have a group mind, a group soul, an egregore that is an intrinsic part of such initiations. Depending upon the circumstances of belief and purpose it may or may not be a prudent choice to seek this route to the Ancestors unless the candidate is suited for the full array of connections and entanglements. Initiation often brings with it a great number of obligations and duties that must be performed on the behalf of the Ancestors and on the behalf of their descendants.

Reincarnation And The Ancestors

Many of the cultures that venerate the Ancestors also believe in some form of reincarnation. How can you call on an Ancestor for assistance when that Ancestor might have returned to the Earth and may be the baby playing on the floor? On the surface this seems an insurmountable paradox, but like most paradoxes, truth is a question of depth. As was pointed out early in this chapter, not everyone who dies merits becoming one of the Ancestors. The vast majority of any given population may be remembered by their friends and loved ones but their deeds do not become local legends. They will be born again and again before they accomplish something truly exemplary. For some readers this may bring to mind the notion that the Ancestors are Ascended Masters or something comparable. That is to say that perhaps these are beings who must no longer be born in flesh to continue their work and evolution. For some small, very small, percentage of the Ancestors this may be true, but for the bulk it is not. The vast majority of people who become Ancestors continue to be reborn and yet their wisdom remains in the unseen realms despite their return to the earth plane. As a related piece of information for those that count souls as if they were keeping accounts and ask where do the extra souls come from to cope with rising populations, the answer is found in the first Hermetic axiom. My phrasing for the axiom is "As above, so below but in a different manner according to its place and time". Reproduction on the physical plane generates more bodies, and reproduction on the astral generates more souls. By extension, procreation on higher planes generates new individualized spirits. So how can we explain the stability of Ancestral presences in the context of the wheel of life, death, and rebirth? For the most part the Ancestors are not individuals nor are they evolving spirits in the way that these are normally understood. The resolution to the paradox is found in examing the nature of the Ancestors.

The Nature Of The Ancestors

The Ancestors of different cultures and peoples will differ in some regards but are generally composed of various proportions of four components: a *summation of shells*, *archetypes*, *collective memory*, and *ensouled group mind*. Although there may be a strong preponderance of one or two of these components in a particular group's Ancestors, all four are present.

Summation Of Shells

Earlier in this chapter, the shedding of the subtle bodies during the process of dying was discussed along with the survival of these shed shells in relationship to ghostly phenomena. These shells contain much of the imprint of what made an individual an individual but are given to decay if not maintained by an external source of energy and cohesion. The shells of those people that are to become part of the Ancestors are collected as they are shed and are woven into the energetic matrix that arises from that community. In this manner they are preserved and more importantly they are made more widely accessible. The source of vitality for these shells is not specific living people, places, or objects but rather the life of the tribe as a whole. This disseminated system for providing vitality removes many of the limits associated with shells. The summation of the shells also refines their wisdom by comparison and cross-linking with all who have come before. This condensation of life experiences underscores the specific social truths of their people, and provides a touchstone for the ethos of the tribe. The shells as individual units do not continue evolving and growing because they are no longer alive but their depth and utility can increase as new shells are added over time. The big picture of the puzzle of life becomes clearer as each piece of life experience is placed.

Archetypes

If an individual has led a life whose experience is worth preserving as one of the Ancestors, there is a high probability that they also have strong affinities to one or more of the archetypes that have meaning in their community. Among other things, the archetypes are the larger than life models for human behavior that are embedded in the collective unconscious of a people. They can be thought of as the much-copied originals for the characters that populate the stage of the world. The archetypes are not just static models, they are also the story arcs and plot-lines associated with enduring truths about the human condition and human nature. Prominent individuals often resemble archetypes in both their character and in their life histories. With varying degrees of conscious awareness, these notable people establish linkages between themselves and the archetypes with whom they are resonant. These linkages persist after death in the traces and links that remain in the shells that have been summed into the Ancestral well of memory. When the Ancestors are called, we not only connect to them but through them to the archetypes that they embodied when they lived. The archetype may use the face of an Ancestor as its interface for communicating with the living.

Collective Memory

That which we call the Ancestors is also one of the clearest and most well defined portals to access the various types of collective memory held by a community. Part of this collective memory is held in the minds of the living members of the community. The doors to these memories are opened to the Ancestors whenever they are called. The Ancestors act as the network and switchboard that transfers these memories. There are also memories from the past that still remain as an imprint upon the fabric of the subtle planes. I am not referring to the Akashic Records in this case but to their stepped down reflection, like a small branch library or a special collection of a larger institution. These imprints contain the memories of all the members of a people, a community, that have died, not just the memories of those that achieved the status of Ancestor. Although theoretically anyone with sufficient psychism and motivation could search the subtle planes for these imprints, it would be as daunting a task as being taken to a huge canyon and hunting for the fossils of a specific family grouping of a species at a particular time. For the Ancestors, anything that is of their metaphorical blood glows with the beacon of filial connection. They can find and relay this information with much greater ease than the living. There is also a third type of collective memory that is the deep, nonverbal, instinctual information that is stored genetically in the DNA and in molecular structures that science has not yet discovered as well in the morphogenetic field of a bloodline which is the subtle and energetic equivalent of genetics. This deep memory can also be accessed with or without the help of the Ancestors but it is easier with their help. The Ancestors are the keepers of the keying pattern to the morphogenetic field.

Ensouled Group Mind

As was explained in the section on dying, one of the reasons that shells degrade is that soul and spirit have disconnected from them. Soul and spirit are the cohesive force and the guiding influence and without them even something as vast as the summed shells of the Ancestors will eventually disintegrate. So where does the soul and spirit come from that is the hub about which turns the pattern that is the Ancestors? Over time the shared thoughts and shared consciousness of the living members of a community create a special and elaborate type of thought form that we call a group mind. This group mind stretches across that which we call the Ancestors. When this group mind achieves sufficient complexity and strength it becomes a suitable habitation for a soul that is overlit by spirit. It may be that this soul is that of some highly evolved human member of that community that chooses to incarnate in the subtle matter of this thoughtform rather than in the dense matter of flesh. Or it may be a high order being from another stream of evolution that is helping to sponsor the growth of that people. It may be something altogether different; regardless of the source for the soul, some things remain true. The thoughtform of the group mind must be be anchored in living members of a community in order to remain a viable vessel for a soul. If all or too many members of a community die, the group mind weakens then dies and the soul must depart. It can be rebuilt but some amount of damage will be done to the summed shells in the absence of a coordinating presence. Recalling the order of the Elements in the Four Worlds of the Qabala, the people are the Earth that supports and feeds the patterns that exist in the subtle Air, the Waters of the soul shape the weather of this Air, and the soul reflects and is moved by the Fire of the spirit.

Divine Embodiment

Most magickal traditions use some form of divine embodiment in their rituals in which a priestess or a priest becomes for a time the vehicle for the presence of one of the Great Ones. This is one of the most intimate and often one of the most powerful ways in which one can directly experience a Great One while incarnate. When it works, it is awe-inspiring, it can act as a great catalyst for change, and is a great validator of spiritual faith. When it fails, and is no more than role playing or ritual theater, it can encourage cynicism, disillusionment, and diminished expectations of what is possible in ritual. When it fails, and there is magick and/or psychism, it can encourage mental imbalance, unwanted personality changes, and sometimes physical illness. In the past, this type of work was generally reserved for the select few that had the temperament, the talent, and the training needed to perform safely and effectively. In recent years the number of people eager to try this form of spiritual contact far exceeds the number of qualified teachers that are available and accessible. This chapter was written with this fact in mind.

I am using the term *divine embodiment* rather than divine possession partly because *possession* is a word that is charged with many connotations, but more importantly because it is only one of the many forms of spirit contact contained within the broader concept of divine embodiment. Divine possession where the will of the priestess or priest is truly subsumed under that of a Great One is rare. In most cases the priestess or priest is awake, aware, and collaborating with the presence that they are embodying. Another important distinction is that possession generally initiates itself and maintains itself whereas in most forms of divine embodiment, the practitioner must strive to create and to hold onto the contact. The simplest definition for divine embodiment is:

> *A state of being created by will and with consent in which an individual anchors into themselves some portion of the energy, information, and essence of a discarnate being of greater stature and/or greater evolution than that of the incarnate individual.*

Before proceeding I would like to point out that there are cultural and religious differences in how the phenomena of divine embodiment occurs. The core perspectives and the basic styles of any given system or tradition are the foundation for the many divergent approaches to divine embodiment. One of the parameters that varies significantly from tradition to tradition is the ratio of the amount of the work done by the individual versus that done by the group. In some modes of divine embodiment the bulk of the energetic and spiritual preparation is done by the group and the group upholds the work of the individual. An example of this is in the mode of divine possession used by the various religions whose roots are Yoruban. This divine possession is made possible by the complex background of intricate drumming, the woven energy of the dancers, and layer upon layer of carefully chosen magickal correspondences. When the Orishas ride their Priestesses and Priests they are very much comparable to soloists singing with a full orchestra. In most of the systems whose roots are in Europe and the Western Magickal Tradition, the individual engaging in divine embodiment is primarily responsible for reaching that state of being. If the divine embodiment is done in a group ritual, the group generally helps to support the work by holding the space and supplementing the energy used to start and maintain the process.

The culturally sanctioned tone and the appropriate manner for relating to the Great Ones can also vary greatly. These differences set the stage for how divine embodiment is experienced and described by the onlookers and the practitioners. Some paths may encourage a deferential posture while others encourage a stance that is almost that of peers. As anyone who has tried to do business overseas knows, what constitutes an insult in one culture may or may not be an insult in another, but attempts at respect are generally recognized. Despite cultural difference, it is a fairly safe bet that if someone is attempting divine embodiment then they have a great deal of respect for the being that they are inviting into their inner selves.

Before coming to any conclusions about the nature of a particular path or tradition method of divine embodiment, ask them about their understanding of what they are doing and if possible observe it for yourself. Sometimes your observations will differ from their descriptions and beliefs and other times you may concur. Sometimes their descriptions and beliefs are on target and sometimes an outsider can see more clearly. Another parameter to consider in the cultural framing of how divine embodiment is done is to see whether the tradition leans more heavily towards a focus on lore, theory, or the way of art. A focus on lore often manifests as an emphasis on memorizing time-proven procedures for divine embodiment and carrying them out to the letter. Generally there is little or no knowledge of the mechanics of how the process works. A focus on theory tends towards greater experimentation with different procedures so long as they match the established theoretical underpinnings. A focus on the way of art results in highly personal approaches that generally work well only for their creator. The goal, as has been stated earlier in this book, is to gain an informed subjectivity in spirit contact and the same applies to an examination of divine embodiment.

Divine embodiment is not the same as channeling, mediumship, mediation, or related practices as these may convey information and guidance but bring very little of the energy and essence of a Great One into a ritual. In divine embodiment, the presence of a Great One within a ritual may contribute energy and power to the work as directly as any of the other participants. The distinction between channeling, etc., and divine embodiment is made for the sake of clarity and not to imply that one is better than the other. Depending upon the setting and the desired outcomes one may be a better choice than the other but they both have intrinsic worth and value. As an example, if you were doing a healing ritual you could have someone channeling very exact diagnoses or suggesting modes of healing. Or you could have someone become the vehicle for a God/dess of healing and have that person perform healing work. The nature of human psyche and human talents makes it highly unlikely that the channeler would have the healing force of a God/dess in their hands. It is as unlikely that a priestess or priest embodying a Great One would be as articulate as a channeler in giving an exact diagnosis. Additionally, individuals may find that they are more suited to one, the other, both, or *neither*.

While it is true that many sincere and spiritually minded practitioners can learn to open and to shape themselves for conveying information or for embodying a Great One, no amount of training or effort will take them beyond their innate potential. It can be said that many people can learn how to sing, but few have the talent to become renown as vocalists. The same is true in metaphysical manners, but it should also be said that many learn well enough to sing for their coven, congregation, or at a friend's wedding. I encourage you to take your development to the fulfillment of your potential, but I also caution you to know your limits. When we are called upon to be vessels for the Great Ones we are doing profoundly sacred work that affects many beings, do not let desires or imaginings cloud your assessment of whether you are prepared and capable. This assessment needs to be done each time we are about to engage in this work as we vary in our competencies and frailties each moment. In manifesting your potential it can be helpful to explore different techniques to find what is best for you. To return to the musical metaphor, make an effort to know what key, what style, and what genre suits the voice that you've been given. A very small number of people have truly broad range and this is true both in octaves and in magick.

Another important variance between practices like that of channeling and that of divine embodiment is evident in the amount of a Great One's essence available for the work at hand. A certain amount of the essence is present in both approaches but the amount is much higher in divine embodiment. In all true channeling there is a certain amount of the essence, without which there would be no context for making sense of the information that is conveyed. One of the marks of excellence in channelers, mediums, and mediators is the amount of essence that they are able to call upon. During divine embodiment, the essence of a Great One, their pattern, becomes anchored within the frame of linear time and becomes one of the sources for the qualities and the attributes of the ritual experience. The essence of a Great One embodied in a ritual permeates the space of the ritual to the same measure that it permeates the person who embodies it.

Techniques & Protocols

There are many techniques and protocols that can be used to achieve divine embodiment. I emphasize the words *techniques* and *protocols* because although it is possible to become a vehicle for divine embodiment without a set pattern or sequence of steps, it is less predictable and often has fewer positive outcomes. There are rare individuals who can do this work with no more than an internal shift of consciousness and a fervent prayer, but they are in the same category as a four year old child who starts playing the piano after watching their mother play. Either they have been gifted with a great talent, have carried the practice and the effort that developed the skill forwards from previous lives, or a bit of both. Unfortunately, it is more common to see individuals displaying some minor or major pathology that masquerades as the Divine. There are also those who confuse a blending of their Waking Self with their Higher Self as the divine embodiment of one of the Great Ones. This is mostly a benign mistake in that the Higher Self is a small spark of the same brilliance that makes up the Great Ones. Challenging circumstances or important moments in time and space can also bring about spontaneous or unbidden divine embodiment. If the Great Ones discern that a crucial nexus is at hand that will help or hinder the unfolding of

Divine Embodiment

some plan or purpose that *matters to them*, they can bring about this sort of divine embodiment. Even with the grave necessity that this suggests, some part of the individual must be ready and willing to give permission. This can, and perhaps should, be called a miracle. Whether or not such permission is conscious depends to a great part on the level of communication between that individual's various parts of self. Discarnate beings that have the power and the will to impose themselves without permission are not the Great Ones I speak of.

    I will touch briefly upon a few of the methods and then describe Aspecting, the method we use in the Assembly of the Sacred Wheel, at length because it is what I know best. Choosing to share the sequence of steps involved in Aspecting required some debate with myself and with some colleagues in the Assembly. In general, the greater the potential effectiveness inherent in a technique, the greater the need for face to face mentoring by a trained practitioner of that technique. This is certainly the case with all the protocols that lead to divine embodiment. Without this type of personalized instruction, there are many real obstacles to success and mastery. Written instructions are easily misunderstood, particularly in the case of esoteric matters where the specialized vocabulary and the context of a tradition carry as much if not more of the real meaning than the words themselves. It is also invaluable to have an outside observer that can give an educated critique of attempts at divine embodiment. Self-delusion is one of the more common obstacles. It is just as easy to believe that a failed attempt has gone splendidly as it is to believe that a successful effort has fallen flat. An outside observer can also make suggestions on how to refine your efforts by scanning your energy. It is difficult to observe your own auric field in detail under normal circumstances and it is exceedingly difficult to do so while juggling the many balls needed to maintain divine embodiment.

    There are also very real risks to both the person attempting divine embodiment and those that are in ritual with that person. A person who is learning to configure themselves to attract and to anchor a divine presence into a ritual will make mistakes. Errors are part of the learning process. A person who is an old hand at divine embodiment will also make errors, though less frequently. When they do make errors, they will manage the errors better and recover more quickly. Another factor to consider is quantity and the quality of mental focus while in a magickal state of consciousness. Although this may improve with practice, people have a finite span of attention and focus. When you are looking closely at something your eyes focus on that one thing. When you are playing a musical instrument, drawing, carving, writing, or engaging in any activity that draws upon multiple resources within your being, other activities and awarenesses are put into the background. You may be aware in a peripheral way of your environment and other tasks but that is all. Most people find that divine embodiment takes up so much of their focus and resources that they have little left to monitor their surroundings let alone to respond quickly and appropriately. Ideally, there should be someone who has a high degree of knowledge about divine embodiment acting as a guardian throughout the ritual. A well planned group ritual often has one or more individuals whose primary duties within that ritual center on keeping the various flows of energy, information, and essence on track and in balance. This not sufficient for rituals that involve divine embodiment. It is best to have someone who has first hand knowledge of what is involved ready to attend to the group or the individuals doing this work.

Many of you reading this will have seen or have gone through unbalancing reactions resulting from powerful rituals; take that up a notch or three and that will give you an inkling of the risks. If matters go sour much of the shock to the system of those in the ritual and those performing divine embodiment occurs in the higher subtle bodies. These higher frequency layers of the aura correspond to higher planes of being which means that it takes longer for the effects to become manifest and easily observable. A very mundane but apt comparison would be that of a sunburn. There are immediate symptoms and then many more that appear as the exposure to too much light ripens and develops. The standard practice of grounding, centering, and the closing of the psychic centers does not address these concerns. Moreover, the smoothing, unruffling, and massaging of a person's aura that is often applied as an intervention to adverse reactions to ritual tends to be effective primarily on the lower subtle bodies. Reparative actions are best performed by someone who has done this type of work before because the energetic patterns that need attention are often neither visible nor intelligible to those that have not experienced divine embodiment. As is true in many magickal concerns, clarity is granted after attainment.

Why I Am Putting This In Print

Unfortunately, there are many more seekers than there are proficient teachers at this time. I for one do not believe that the conventional wisdom of "when the student is ready, the teacher will appear" is valid during the tumult and turbulence of the turning of an Age. During the transition from one astrological age to another, a large number of people are drawn to spiritual pursuits. This is nature's way of exploring all the possibilities for the shape of the things for the new age. It is not unlike a baby boom where the young greatly outnumber the old and which tends to open the doors to profound transformation. In these times of change, nature takes great risks therefore it seems justified to take the risk of sharing information that under other circumstances would only be shared from mouth to ear.

Drawing Down The Moon & Drawing Down The Sun

In the Neo-Pagan community one of the better known forms of divine embodiment is known as the drawing down the Moon. Drawing down of the moon refers to calling the Goddess into a priestess. There is also the practice called drawing down of the Sun which refers to calling the God into a priest. This mode of divine embodiment has its origins in the Wiccan community but has been generalized to the broader Neo-Pagan community. When it is done well it is a glorious thing to experience but because there is an expectation that the drawing down should be included in many rituals for the sake of form, it is often performed in a watered-down fashion.

The Drawing Down process brings the presence of a Deity into the subtle bodies of an individual. As the name for this mode of divine embodiment would imply, the Great One is pulled deeper and deeper into the layers of the person's aura until sufficient presence is invested in the person in order to function within that person's consciousness. This can be imagined or visualized as a fluid pouring down from above and filling layer upon layer of the aura. This also means that the chakras are activated and engaged beginning with the transpersonal, then the Crown, and so forth following the central column of energy flow. The passage of the energy, information, and essence of the great one that is being drawn down is linear and procedural. The attributes of the great one that is being drawn down relates directly to the state of being of each of the chakras and each subtle body. To better understand this process, meditate upon what you know about the process of incarnation, the downward journey of the flash in the tree of life, or any other system that describes manifestation.

Certainly no living being can contain or encompass a Great One's energy field. What is possible is that a portion of that Great One's presence can lodge within each layer of the aura. Like calls to like even if the pattern is separated by octaves of difference. Those things that are far beyond our knowledge that are the equivalent of the subtle bodies of a Great One seek their counterpart within the human's subtle bodies. Understanding the mechanism for how drawing down works reveals why it is very effective for some people and less so for others. Firstly, the individual must be willing and able to set aside their resistance which would exclude the entry of the certain parts of the Great One into their energy field. This resistance is not a singular thing but a complex of things. Generally there are varying degrees of openness and a resistance at each layer within each subtle body. I remind you that these qualities of openness and resistance are constantly in flux and depend upon all factors that shape the person's state of being. Beyond simple resistance, there is also the question of the holding capacity of each of the layers and each of the subtle bodies.

Although it is implied in what I just said, psychological factors strongly affect what is possible for any given person attempting to find embodiment through the drawing down process. Issues of intimacy, vulnerability, trust, and safety are perhaps the most important to consider in this regard. Some of the differences in openness and resistance arise from the influences of gender, socialization, and sexuality upon the very intimate co-mingling of selves that is part and parcel of Drawing Down.

The mechanism of the Drawing Down process also explains why certain individuals will have greater or lesser capacity in working with particular goddesses or gods. Each individual has the unique mixture of energies in patterns that mirror a variety of the Great Ones. As a result, in the Drawing Down process that unique mixture of energies in patterns will act as an antenna that will receive or reject those frequencies or waveforms that suit its shape. This is a metaphor and I don't mean to suggest that it is as simple as that, but it is a solid comparison. An FM antenna does not pick up AM signals very well . Similarly, the resonance that a person has to particular archetypes, mythic themes, emotions, and stages of life impact greatly on the specifics of their receptivity.

In addition to resonance, the Drawing Down process also uses polarity. The person attempting this form of divine embodiment will have lowered their resistance and opened themselves but this in and of itself will not draw the Divine Presence down into the lower planes which correspond to the lower subtle bodies. It is essential that this occur if there is to be useful communication and significant interaction. This is where the use of polarity provides the active component to balance the passive receptive component of Drawing Down. In traditional Wicca this is usually accomplished through the use of polarity as expressed by a male/female dyad. A woman draws the

Sun (God) into a man, and a man draws the Moon (Goddess) into a woman. Through invocations, energy work, dance or other forms of motion the presence of a Great One is pulled into the person. This can be thought of as a magnetic attraction or the application of suction to start a siphon. If the Great One that is to be Drawn Down has a gender association, then the person doing the invoking and pulling should ideally be of the opposite gender. This is not the only way, but in many ways it is easier. Although the dyad of priestess and priest is the classic expression of the Drawing Down process, it works just as well with the group as a whole providing the pull to call the Great One into a human vessel. This also expands the concept of polarity, in that there is a contrast between an individual and a group which of itself will cause energy to flow.

Despite certain dogmas and doctrines, Drawing Down is practiced quite effectively in many women's spirituality groups, Dianic Wiccan covens, or other single gender settings. Polarity is not simply a matter of female and male. There are three readily accessible sources for polarity that can be used in single gender groups or for solo work. These three modes of polarity provide the current, the flow, that brings the Great One down into the person. In this context I am speaking of the Drawing Down process but as you'll see, these forms of polarity are also at play in other protocols for divine embodiment. It has been my experience that these modes of polarity work whether or not the practitioners are fully aware of how they are accomplishing the divine embodiment.

Microcosm — Macrocosm

There is a strong bond that connects the microcosm to the macrocosm, the below to the above. This is the preeminent teaching in Hermetics. If the practitioner enters into a deep state of intense identification with the Great One that they would embody, they activate a polarity with the macrocosm that corresponds to that Great One. Each human being is a microcosm of the Whole and theoretically can find within themselves the resources to shape themselves into a microcosm that is a specific below that corresponds to a specific above. Like calls to like, and the small and the large are drawn towards becoming one.

Linear Time — Eternity

Another source polarity that is inherent in all humans is that which exists between linear time and nonlinear time (eternity). Though we may live in linear time, it is rare for us to be truly as aware of this as we are of our location in space. Many wise people have extolled the value of living in the Now, the present, and there are many wholesome spiritual and psychological consequences from doing so, but there can also be magickal implications. One of the truths about polarities is that the further towards the extremes you approach, the more similarities between the so-called opposites are encountered. Our normal waking consciousness jitters and skips back and forth between the just past and the about to be. Normal waking consciousness hovers in a cloud of probability that surrounds the now. In part this is a consequence of the neurology of sensory perception and in part it is the result of our awareness catching up with or anticipating external reality. With effort it is possible to shrink and to thin the cloud that surrounds the Now. It is possible to control the motion of our consciousness so that it cleaves more closely to that dimensionless point that is the Now. When that is done, then there is a strongly polarized bond between linear time and eternity. It is a more perfect expression of the vitalizing tension that comes from a complementary grouping of similarities and differences. Meditate on both the image of a circle with a dot at its center as well as their definitions, seeing the forms respectively as eternity and linear time.

Gender — Meta-Gender

Gender covers an assortment of possibilities and patterns of interrelationship which can constitute polarity. I am using the term "gender" in a sweeping manner inclusive of many possibilities. Gender combines with identity, culture, roles, appearance, biology, behavior, and a myriad of other factors to become evident. Gender only exists within a context, within relationships, and within comparisons. Like water, gender is shaped by its container, the characteristics of its motion, and is the color that it reflects. It is said that every human contains male and female qualities, though most humans generally are represented as one or the other. It is also said that the Great Ones are beyond gender, yet many are represented as having a distinct gender. This attribution of gender to the Great Ones may be a concession to the limits of human understanding, but it must also contain a kernel of truth. The gender of a Great One is perhaps better thought of as a meta-gender that includes all the potentialities of gender but with the capacity to express one, many, or all of those potentials. In addition to the readily seen polarity of complementary opposites, there are two more recondite polarities based in gender that can occur between a human and a Great One. One is comparable to the polarity of the microcosm to the macrocosm in that human's gender is a small reflection of the greater form of gender expressed in a Great One. The other form is comparable to the polarity of linear time to eternity in that human gender and meta-gender, that includes all potentialities, are the same phenomena acting within different frames of reference.

Regardless of the mechanism of action used in producing the Drawing Down, the result is that the energy, information, and essence of the Great One molds itself to the contours and limits of the subtle bodies of the person. This method makes for ease of interaction with the Great One because it has been translated into the form of the human vessel. In so doing, it becomes more intelligible to us, but the size and power of the presence is truncated by this process. A person who has drawn down a Goddess or a God will be able to speak, move, and participate in a ritual with relative ease. However, the amount present, for lack of a better term, of that Goddess or God can be no more than that person's best effort. You cannot pour an ocean into a teaspoon; a person's capacity is finite. Like all forms of divine embodiment, one of the healthy consequences of its practice is the growth of the individual. Just as lung capacity can be increased by deep breathing exercises, the capacity to hold a portion of a Great One can also be increased which means the person has become more than they were before.

The Assumption of God Forms

The Assumption of God Forms is a technique from the Ceremonial current of Western Magick to accomplish divine embodiment. There are a number of different protocols for Assumption, each tailored in a way that fits the purposes and the beliefs of the traditions that created them. There are commonalities between these and I will focus on them in these descriptions. Assumption can also be used for the embodiment of beings other than Deities though that is its primary use. The person builds up a thought form, an astral construct, that corresponds to the Deity Form. This is often done through visualizing an image of the Deity that is richly packed with its archetypal attributes, by vibrating its sacred name, and scribing a the sigil or symbol of that Form. The person sends out a call to the furthest reaches of the universe, and if all is well the call is answered. The Deity approaches and the person's subtle bodies are enfolded and encapsulated within the larger Deity form. The person acts as the magnet/anchor that allows an eternal being to hover within the frame of time. The image of a fancifully shaped balloon from the Macy's Thanksgiving parade being pulled by a tether is not far off the mark. This technique brings a greater part of the Deity form into a ritual but does not create the ease of interaction between the person and the Deity form experienced in Drawing Down. In Assumption, a person's subtle bodies are not filled by the presence of a Great One. In Assumption, the Great One affects the person by the indirect means of resonance and induction while having a direct effect on the space of the ritual by virtue of being held in synchronization with linear time by the anchor of an incarnate human. Since Assumption does not truncate the Great One to the limits of a human vessel, a greater amount of the presence can be called upon. Regrettably, this also means that the Great One is not translated into human terms which makes communication and collaboration more arduous.

Assumption relies upon many of the same mechanisms, sources of cohesion, and polarities that are used in Drawing Down. The differences come from the form that the divine embodiment takes. In Drawing Down, the intensity and the degree of efficacy is on a fairly smooth continuum that spans the range of the person's capacity. In Assumption, there are three distinct continua with ranges of efficacy that are distinct to each. You may think of these like the gears in a car or a bicycle, each with preferred speeds and preferred road conditions.

In the first grade of Assumption, the archetypal image that is built up by the practitioner becomes energized in each level of the practitioner's being. Visualization, or more fully realization, is a powerful thing in and of itself but even the first grade of Assumption is more than that. When the image of the Great One finds its own analogous part in the Higher Self of the practitioner, then we have crossed the line between imagining and being. At the highest point of the first grade, what hovers over the practitioner is their Higher Self, their Divine Self, transfigured to the form of the Great One that they have called.

In the second grade of Assumption, the call reaches beyond the boundary of the individual practitioner and connects the transfigured Higher Self to the Archetype, the Form, of the Great One they have called. When this bridging between the individual and the collective occurs, the type of Assumption that is necessary for effective work in ritual begins. In the second grade of Assumption, the practitioner has brought more than what they are into play. At the highest point of the second grade, what hovers over the practitioner is the repository of all that has been offered by humans in the elaboration of that Form through the Ages.

Divine Embodiment

In the third grade of Assumption, the image, the Archetype, has been so energized and so awakened as to call the attention of the Great One that is being sought. The Great One then connects to the Form which is in turn connected to the Higher Self of the practitioner. This can be imagined as a Great One taking its place upon its throne or wrapping about itself its mantle of office. When this occurs, the Great One is truly and fully present. At the highest point of the third grade, there is a chain of connection that reaches from the human to the Divine.

You may have noticed that the descriptions for these three grades of Assumption each mention what is possible at the highest point of that grade. This does not mean that you must reach the highest point of a grade to enter in to the next. There are grades and there are grades. As is true of schools, only passing marks are required to move to the next grade. It is also true that how well one does may vary from grade to grade. Another resonance to the pattern of school work is that what is learned in one grade lays the foundation for the next. Thankfully, in the case of Assumption, we get to try our hand at improving our marks each time we try. The qualities and efficacy of any given foray into Assumption is set by what is accomplished at each grade. Excellence in Assumption is an aggregation of the efforts at each grade. I have observed that the desire for achievement often pushes people to reach higher than they are ready. In ritual, I would rather experience someone displaying the highest point of the first grade of Assumption than a mediocre rendition of the third grade. I would rather hear a modest song sung with grace than hear a voice straining through the range of a difficult song.

As is true within most traditions and communities, terms can be used loosely or become generalized as a quick description. I have been to a number of rituals of the Ceremonial flavor where there was a need for more people to fill ritual roles that required Assumption than there were trained candidates. Under those circumstances, a highly talented and trained initiate can invest the mantle of divine embodiment onto untrained albeit willing participants. The effect on the participants and on the ritual is similar to Assumption and it will often be labeled Assumption. There is more than one way to do this. I will describe the most common one. It differs from a thoroughgoing Assumption in that the form of the Great One is built up externally by the initiate and then placed into the participant. Then the Great One is pulled down into the participant in a manner similar to Drawing Down. Since the participant does not take as active a role in the process of building up the form or calling the Great One the effect is not as strong as full-fledged Assumption, but it is often more than enough for the tasks at hand.

Divine Possession

I have witnessed but not directly experienced Divine Possession as I am defining it in this chapter. Certainly the more complete, the more extreme manifestations of any of the techniques I am describing may appear to be Divine Possession, but there are some important differences. The most important functional difference is that the Great One that is called generally initiates the possession and maintains it. The practitioner in Divine Possession will have worked to prepare themselves, will have opened themselves and will have made the offer but thereafter their role is mostly passive. Another crucial distinction is that the practitioner cannot break the connection. They remain in the state of divine possession until: they are released, their subtle bodies and physical body are exhausted, or someone else breaks the connection. This type of divine embodiment generally only takes place in a strongly focused religious context. There is a great deal of trust, adoration, and devotion required for divine possession to work well and to work smoothly. It is rare for this level of veneration to exist outside of a focused religious context. By a focused religious context, I mean a committed worship of a specific pantheon or of a specific God or Goddess long enough to form a deeply personal relationship. As an example, you cannot have a deeply personal relationship with the Moon Goddess, but you can with Artemis or Selene. Let me give an example from mundane human life that clarifies this point. Being in love with a person is not the same as being in love with the idea of love. Intimacy requires a true meeting of authentic selves. There is little that can be imagined that is more intimate than Divine Possession. There is also perhaps no greater violation than possession without consent which is anything but divine. Divine Possession is most commonly practiced in cultures and communities where religion and magick have not diverged from each other. When the intellectual and emotional distance between religion, spirituality, and magick is small, the distance to the Great Ones is small as well. One of the practical effects in ritual is that the relative distance and the subjective divisions between the planes of being are greatly reduced. This facilitates the mechanism by which Divine Possession is accomplished.

My observation of Divine Possession has been through Native American rituals and through the Yoruban rooted traditions of which Santeria is one. I am fortunate to be gifted with keen psychic sight and I have focused that

Divine Embodiment

gift on people during divine possession. Energetically, Divine Possession resembles Drawing Down more than it resembles Assumption. The Great One enters into the practitioner and fills their subtle bodies but in a very different manner than Drawing Down. In Divine Possession, the Great One that has been called, interleaves themselves into the subtle bodies of the practitioner like two decks of cards being shuffled into one. It looks like a sideways step into the person. Rather than pouring down through the Crown Chakra and filling the central energy column, the Great One creates a space where there was no space before. The Great One fills these spaces between each layer of the person's aura, each subtle body. The Great One then controls the flow of energy, information, and essence in both the direction that moves in and out of the Chakras between the layers of the subtle body and also the flow that runs up and down the central energy column. This allows them to act almost as if they were incarnate, as a temporary avatar.

The practitioner of Divine Possession often has little or no control over their actions and often a very unclear recollection of the experience. This is an outcome of the mechanism of Divine Possession. By interleaving themselves throughout the practitioner, the Great One becomes the primary neural network, the seat of consciousness, for the duration of the Possession. In Voudoun, the Great Ones, the Orishas, are seen as Divine Horsemen and the Priestess or Priest is mounted by them. Let's ride this imagery. The horse does not partake of the consciousness of the rider, nor does the rider experience the consciousness of the horse, but over time a deep symbiotic relationship can develop. The horse and the rider can at first anticipate each other and then with time can act as one. Divine Possession is a very special and temporary incarnation, but the rules of incarnation still apply. When humans are born, their spirits must learn how to use the vehicle of the body, and the body must learn to respond to those requests. An infant learns to see, to walk, and ultimately to talk. The Great Ones that engage in Divine Possession are much more than human, but they too must develop a relationship with the body and its resident soul and spirit. Conversely, the human must learn to respond to the requests and directions of the Great One. It is hardly surprising that we often see jerky motions, staggering, odd vocalizations, and slurred speech in Divine Possession. What is surprising is that there are practitioners who can progress to high levels of physical coordination and verbal facility. When the Divine Possession does not go smoothly and the various subtle bodies are not properly interleaved, all sorts of chaos can result. Depending upon the particulars, the practitioner, and the Great One that is called, Divine Possession can be sublime, farcical, or frightening. One thing remains true regardless of the circumstances, in Divine Possession the presence is undeniable.

Each of the modes for divine embodiment have their strengths and their weaknesses. Although a certain amount of innate talent is required for all these methods, Divine Possession requires a substantial natural talent and a very flexible psyche. Training can never create talent nor aptitudes, it can only develop them. I have seen many examples of divine embodiment in many rituals from many traditions. I have only seen what I would call a Living God or a Living Goddess in Divine Possession. Sadly, as is true for all of these methods, the upper reaches of what is possible rarely occurs. This is more true for Divine Possession, as its prerequisites are higher.

You may notice that I am not giving you word one on how to accomplish Divine Possession. You cannot reverse engineer nor can you extrapolate how it is done from my description of the energetic mechanism. If you feel that you have the strength, the gift, and the temperament, find your way to a House or a Medicine Society or some other traditional system. See if you have the calling to merge your path, religion, and magick into an existing and deep rooted tradition. If you cannot conform and adapt, then this is not for you. While you may be able to safely experiment with a variety of rituals and techniques from the many branches of the Western Magcikal Traditions, you cannot trifle with Divine Possession.

Some of you may say, "But I've already experienced it!" and indeed I have heard this comment in my classes. When I hear this, I certainly believe that the person has had a meaningful experience, but I do not accept their interpretation unless there is a considerable amount of corroboration. It is easy to mistake a strong experience with one of the other forms of divine embodiment with Divine Possession. I have also heard similar comments in regards to overshadowing and the even rarer indwelling. My guess is that in many cases this is a result of insufficient exposure or experience of these phenomena or what I call the health class effect. At some point in your educational career, you probably had a mandatory health class that you attended. I had a friend in High School who was concerned that they might have a venereal disease despite the fact they were a virgin. As they listened to the symptoms of illnesses in these classes, many people decide that they have them. Another possibility is that people want to magnify the nature of their spiritual and magickal experiences to gain validation and to bolster self-esteem.

Aspecting

In 1986 I was moved to create a protocol for divine embodiment that would be more suited to the form of Wicca that was practiced by my coven, Keepers of the Holly Chalice. Keepers is the coven that was the seed for the Assembly of the Sacred Wheel. The form of Wicca that the Assembly practices is syncretic and draws inspiration from Astrology, Qabala, the Western Magickal Tradition and the folk religions of Europe. We had used the more traditionally Wiccan Drawing Down method in our rituals, but found that it was not the right tool for all our rituals. My process for creating the protocol involved art, science, and craft. Through visioning, contemplating, and mediating I would create drafts that I would then subject to thought experiments and then actual experimentation. After I had polished and tested the protocol well enough to feel that it was safe and effective, I shared it with my coven. Aspecting, as I will teach it in this chapter, has proven itself over the years to be quite effective both in the Assembly and with others who have adopted it as one of their tools. In addition to being an attempt to span a broader reach of the Western Magickal Tradition, Aspecting was also designed to be as safe as any method of divine embodiment can be.

I would like to acknowledge the spirits and the coven mates that helped me in the process of creating and refining Aspecting. I would also like to acknowledge that this protocol is also influenced by ideas and techniques from: Wicca of the Farrar flavor; the Western Magickal Tradition of primarily the Golden Dawn style; the works of Dolores Ashcroft-Nowicki, Murry Hope, Marion Weinstein, and Roger Zelazny's fiction. No doubt there are others worthy of thanks and mention but creativity and invention rarely have clear provenance and straightforward genealogy.

As a point of clarification, the term aspecting is also used by the Reclaiming Tradition of witchcraft. Exactly what they mean by aspecting and how they do it has as many explanations as there are Reclaiming witches. The elder part of the roots of Reclaiming's magick is from the Feri Tradition of Victor and Cora Anderson and has within it the wildness one would expect of Faerie. Reclaiming leans more towards the way of Art and is often ecstatic and spontaneous. My experience of their aspecting affirms this mutability. Their aspecting often resembles Drawing Down with a dash of shamanic trance work. I have also seen it act more like a form of Assumption wherein the Form is expanded by a sort of turning of the Self until only that facet of the Self which resembles the Great One that is being called is prominent. Moreover, it is other combinations of methods as well. The uniting thread in what I have seen is that it is protean, primal, and still in flux as a method. It does work, don't mistake my comments as a disparagement, it is just not my place to impose the assertion of a pattern on a method that is still unfolding.

Aspecting as it is done by the Assembly of the Sacred Wheel combines some of the characteristics of Drawing Down and Assumption with some additional steps. Both male and female polarities are activated within the practitioner to give the option of calling a Great One of either the same or the opposite gender of the practitioner. There is also an activation of the macrocosm - microcosm resonance as well as the special polarity between time - eternity. A portion of the Great One being Aspected enters into the energy field of the practitioner and another portion remains just above the bounds of the subtle bodies. The bulk of the interaction between the Great One and the practitioner is mediated through the individual's Higher Self. Although the Higher Self of the practitioner has the leading role in this protocol; the Lower and Middle Selves are active partners in making Aspecting work. For those of you who analyze things in terms of the Qabala, you may think of Aspecting as led by the Neschamah, fueled by the Nephesch, and implemented by the Ruach.

Combining elements of Drawing Down, Assumption of God Forms, and techniques to integrate the various Parts of Self does create a dynamic that reduces some of the problems inherent in these methods but it does not eliminate all the drawbacks. In fact it has shortcomings that are unique to its own mechanisms of action. Each method of divine embodiment that I am describing is like any other tool, good at what it is meant to do. A small sharp knife may be just the thing for intricate carving but you wouldn't think to use it for cutting lumber to frame a house. Aspecting is like a power tool with an assortment of attachments, you have to know which attachment to pick and how to work within the limits of the motor's power.

The efficacy of this technique hinges on the quality of the link between the various Parts of Self and the amount of the practitioner's incorporated magickal knowledge. By "incorporated", I mean fully woven into the subtle bodies so that skills, sequences of actions, and powers can be summoned with no more expenditure of effort than that of a typist's fingers knowing the way to convert thought to text. Aspecting works best with people who do magick and ritual on a regular basis. Reading about magick, even in-depth study, does not incorporate magick into the subtle bodies anymore than reading about a musical instrument will allow you to play it. Aspecting does not favor the armchair occultist or the weekend warrior. Even after a person has become proficient in Aspecting, they must be in shape, properly conditioned, for it to work well. There must also be a strong and coordinated linkage between the various Parts of Self. Without this coherence, this coadunation, of Selves there is a tendency to drop out of Aspect or to become unfocused. A strong will is needed to keep the many elements of this technique balanced and energized. This is not an easy technique, but it has the potential to be both very effective in divine embodiment and in strengthening and enriching the practitioner.

As in Assumption, there are identifiable grades or levels of Aspecting. In Assumption, the grades correspond to a linkage of three progressively larger states of being. There are four levels of Aspecting. There are four because they correspond to the planes of existence that are called the Four Worlds in the Qabala. These four Planes can also be thought of as the foundations that uphold all cyclical phenomena, and the process of the Four Elements.

At the first level of Aspecting, the Great One's presence can be felt within the ritual space by those who are sensitive. The practitioner's voice, gestures, and carriage will have changed enough so that it is evident to almost anyone that a Great One is within them. Those who are sensitive or have the sight will perceive that the energy of the practitioner will have changed as well. At this level of Aspecting the practitioner and participants often experience a sharpening of the senses, colors and sounds will seem richer and more distinct. The Great One's words come easily and fluently through the lips of the practitioner. The power worked in the ritual feels mostly human in origin, but it has a luster and a finish that is more than human. The Great One edits, refines, and adjusts what has been wrought to bring it to its peak without adding anything that wasn't already there.

When taken to its greatest intensity, the first level of Aspecting exalts the senses and reveals the world for the enchantment that it is.

At the second level of Aspecting, the Great One's presence within the ritual is felt by most people because time seems to flow at a variable rate and light and sound are somewhat distorted. The practitioner radiates power and they look physically different to most people. The practitioner will often feel tingling in their bodies and they will feel that their size or shape has changed. When the Great One speaks through them, the words come less easily but are filled with more meaning. Words spoken in Aspect at this level carry information and multiple levels. I do not merely mean that they are packed with allusions or metaphors. Some participants may see images or hear non vocalized messages that accompany the words. At the second level, the ritual has a wide strand of power woven into it that is clearly from the Great One.

When taken to its greatest intensity, the second level of Aspecting truly takes us between the worlds in fact, not just in words.

At the third level of Aspecting, other realities seem to overlay the ritual space. Generally, there is less distinction between what is grasped by the physical senses and what is perceived by the subtle senses. This causes the variability of what is experienced by everyone involved in the ritual to rise. Although every individual's experience of a ritual is unique, at this level of Aspecting the differences are more pronounced. There is also a greater separation in the experience of the practitioner and the experience of the participants. The practitioner may feel strongly disconnected from their body and may experience a dimming of their senses. Their bodies may feel thick and slow moving, though others observe no changes. They may report that their memories of the Aspecting are disjointed or unclear. This murkiness of consciousness is not inherent to this level of Aspecting, rather it is a marker for the condition of the practitioner. If you are unaccustomed to mountain climbing you may find yourself out of breath and lightheaded, while a veteran climber seems not to notice the altitude at all. When waking consciousness is raised to a higher level than it is acclimated, it fades while higher consciousness continues to operate. With effort and adaptation this situation can be alleviated. When this adaptation is accomplished, the magick of thought becoming manifestation can be shepherded from plane to plane with ease.

When taken to its greatest intensity, the third level of Aspecting truly reduces the distance between the planes of being so that the worlds touch and blend.

The fourth level of Aspecting rarely occurs. When it does occur it is a sublime harmonization that makes the many planes and worlds seem truly one. The participants experience the highest expression of what they are capable of at that time, in that ritual. The practitioner's senses and psychic centers are fully opened and they perceive many levels at once as if with many eyes. Their consciousness is profoundly coupled with that of the Great One that they are Aspecting. I have yet to meet anyone who can maintain this level for more than a handful of minutes. If the fourth level is achieved, even for a few seconds, the practitioner can then continue at the third level with greater clarity.

The fourth level of Aspecting, when it occurs, shows us what is possible.

In Drawing Down and in Assumption, the intensity, grade, or level remains relatively constant after the divine embodiment has been established and stabilized. In Aspecting the level can vary throughout the entire attempt. This is one of the benefits and one of the drawbacks of Aspecting as a method of divine embodiment. It can be compared to flying; work is required to get aloft and to remain aloft. Furthermore, different species of birds fly in styles suited to their wings and their weather.

The Aspecting Protocol

The following is an outline of the steps required to go into Aspect. The outline assumes the reader is familiar with certain ideas and techniques. If you find something that is unfamiliar to you, check to see if it is covered in this book and if it is not, do some research. After reading the outline you may wish to re-read the description of Aspecting for new insights. If you intend to try this protocol, I suggest after a thorough study of it that you have a trusted magickal colleague guide you through the steps in numerous short practice sessions. It is important that your first attempts at Aspecting be brief with progressively longer efforts. Think of this the way you would think of athletic training. Push yourself but also allow your subtle bodies time to strengthen and gain flexibility between sessions. You can over-train and you can also lose ground if you wait too long between efforts. When you are practicing Aspecting, you need not pour your all into each attempt. Like a dancer learning new choreography or a singer learning a new song, the form is learned before passion and power can flow at their fullest.

A number of the people that I have taught to Aspect have asked me about the propriety of calling a Great One for a practice session. I am in agreement with the many teachers that warn to always raise power for a valid purpose and to treat the Great Ones with respect. When you practice Aspecting or any other form of divine embodiment, you must remember why you have called upon a Great One. Practice is a request to be prepared for service. Practice also encourages your personal evolution through your exertion and through your contact with the essence of a Great One. These are valid reasons to call upon a Great One. It has also been my experience that the Great Ones only send as much of themselves as is needed for the purpose at hand. The spirit in which you enter into practice very much determines the Spirit that enters into you.

I. Ground & Center

    A. Turn your focus of attention inwards. Become aware of the central channel, the column of energy that runs in alignment with your spine. Become aware of it in much the way that you would become aware of the beating of your heart and the movement of your breath. Intensify this awareness of the central column through the use of imagery. The easiest way to do this is by visualizing a tree whose trunk is your spine. This tree's roots delve downwards from your feet and its branches rise from your shoulders and head towards the heavens. If you are indoors, make certain that the tree extends through the floor and through the roof. Once the central column is solidly a part of your awareness, extend your perception to include the many flows of energy that move up and down the column. Depending upon your beliefs and temperament, you will perceive the flows in different ways. Although this step can be done in any posture, it is best to do so while standing or while sitting with a straight back.

B.   Now find the place within yourself that is the focus of your consciousness, of your Self. For most people, this beginning location is in a place in their heads just behind the eyes. Try to concentrate your focus of consciousness into a small sphere. Use your will to gently rock your focus of consciousness back and forth until it drifts free. Let your consciousness drift up and down within the central column. Allow it to move until it finds its own center of balance within the column. Don't let preconceptions force it into the location you believe to be correct. In most cases it will find its resting place somewhere between the throat and the navel. The exact location will vary from attempt to attempt because you will be different. Comparable to the center of gravity, this is the center of consciousness.

• *Grounding and centering helps to prepare you for the fluctuations in power as the Aspecting is established and helps later on in its maintenance. Until the third step in the process of going into Aspect, there will be moments of real imbalance and dissonance. If you are aware of blockages, misalignments, or problems associated with your subtle bodies or particular chakras, it would be wise to work on them before beginning any attempt at Aspecting. It is especially important that the central column through which the bulk of the energy, information, and essence will flow is clear. Concentrating the focus of consciousness, preparing it for motion, and finding its balance point provide another sort of anchoring and grounding in setting the bounds for the work that follows.*

II. Call The Five Parts Of Self Into Harmony

A.   This step involves the use of the Tattva symbols as keys for the Elements, their associated Part of Self, and the subtle bodies associated with the planes of existence that are related to the Four World in the Qabala. In this protocol, the association for Ether, the Quintessence, is seen as being present in all the Elements and as the boundary that contains them as well. If you are not familiar with these symbols please read the appendix on the Tattvas before continuing.

Body	Earth	A Yellow Square
Mind	Air	A Blue Circle
Heart	Water	A Silver Crescent
Soul	Fire	A Red Triangle
Spirit	Ether	A Clear Egg Or Oval

Call forth these symbols in your mind's eye to activate them in your consciousness and meditate briefly upon them before starting the next phase of this step. It has been my experience that maintaining the distinction between soul and spirit is difficult for many people. The soul is the part of your essence that evolves through the lessons of your current incarnation; it is immanent from this life. The spirit is the part of you that is eternal and is the summation of you that exists outside of linear time; it is transcendent. In this system of categorizing the Parts of Self, spirit can be though of as being the Higher Self, Divine Self, or the Holy Guardian Angel in ceremonial terms.

B. Visualize and affirm the meanings of the the Yellow Square and place it at the center of consciousness that you found in the first step. Then repeat the process for the Blue Circle, the Silver Crescent, the Red Triangle, and lastly the Egg of Spirit. Visualize these geometric forms as being placed upon the center of consciousness in concentric fashion as if they were badges. The shapes may be of the same size or may be gradually smaller. If you have great ease of visualization, you may see these as three dimensional forms. As a tool for incorporating this step into your knowledge you may wish to cut the shapes in their appropriate colors out of paper or felt and place them upon each other as you practice. Another possibility is to cut the shapes from stronger materials and string them on a cord in their order. With your eyes shut, you can finger the shapes as you experience them in your mind.

- *This step more than the others determines the amount of the Great One that will be brought into your energy field, and how much will be left anchored above you. The process of working with symbols that are correlated to the Elements, to Parts of Self, and to the planes of being helps to bring the subtle bodies into alignment. If you like you may add the visualization of the various subtle bodies aligning evenly inside each other like Russian nesting dolls. Reaffirming the inherent or-*

der of the Parts of Self also helps to clarify your conscious mind's link to your Higher Self. Communication between the conscious mind and the Higher Self is most easily achieved through nonverbal means. One of the effects of bolstering your center of consciousness with these charged symbols, charged both with energy and with purpose, is a stabilization of that center so that it remains as an anchor throughout the Aspecting. The fixing of your attention upon your center of consciousness also helps to dilate the central column of energy into which a portion of the Great One will flow.

III. Calling The Balance Of Goddess & God

A. Call upon your name(s) to affirm your selfhood, aloud or silently. This may be one name or it may be a short list of names. This list can include magickal names, spirit names, your maiden name, family or clan names, or other names that help you to declare your identity.

B. Proclaim yourself as an aspect of God or Goddess incarnate. If you are a woman, your body is a part of the Goddess made flesh. If you are a man, your body is a part of the God made flesh. If you are transgendered, determine for yourself whether it is Goddess, God or both that is expressed in your flesh. Proclaim yourself as an embodiment of Goddess or God. If you have a particular God or Goddess that is your patron, name them. If you do not, then say it in the more abstracted form of Goddess or God. Then call upon the Deity of the opposite gender that you have a connection with and declare a harmonious relation. If you have several Gods and Goddesses with whom you truly have a profound relationship, you may name them as well. However you should be mindful of not naming God/dess/es whose energies would clash with the Great One that is to be Aspected. You may simplify this step by just naming the Goddess or God you are about to Aspect and a compatible opposite gender Deity, but this doesn't give you as much support.

- *This is the step that is the most variable. It is important that careful thought be given to selecting the name or names that are said in affirming your identity. You must reinforce your concept of identity, and if you have developed a magickal persona, activate that as well. Do not use a magickal name just because you think you should have one. If it is not a magickal name that you have claimed through an initiation, a vision, or some other serious process, then it probably does not add to this step and it may detract. This part of the step helps to generate a sense of security and solidity that is essential to Aspecting. If your boundaries are clear, there is less threat in sharing yourself with a Great One. It will also be easier to disengage from the Aspecting when you are done. Kindling the light of your au-*

thentic identity also sparks the power needed to awaken the resonances that you have with the Divine Feminine and the Divine Masculine. Identifying with Goddess and God balances and energizes your gender polarities to secure additional energy for this working. The calling also brings the protection, assistance, and guidance afforded by patron Deities. Do not play at having patrons, if you do not have a personal relationship with a Great One do not pretend to it. Reading about a particular Goddess or God and seeing a piece of them within you is not enough. You are not riding on coattails, you are taking the hand of a beloved. Like any intimate relationship, there is a consensual mutual claiming after a course of discoveries. This step works well enough with a more general call to the Goddess and the God, if you don't have specific patrons. Because perspectives and approaches to the concept of identity and to connection to the Divine are deeply personal and hence wildly variable, this step is the one that is modified more than the others. As you make alterations to this step to fit you, bear in mind the purposes of this step.

IV. **Naming What You Would Aspect**

A. Name aloud the particular Great One or facet of a Great One that you would Aspect. It is important that you say it aloud even if circumstances require that you whisper it. The goal is to have each of your subtle bodies utter that name on their corresponding planes of being. Your physical body must also speak the name as well to complete the sequence.

B. If you have an image of what the Great One looks like, see it in your mind's eye. This image may be the historical or traditional representation of the Great One, your personal vision of them, or some blending of these. Then allow the image to transform or morph into a simple icon that represents the Great One. Then place this icon over the oval, the egg of Spirit, at your center of consciousness. It is very important that you be specific. There is much greater presence if you call on Diana than if you call on the Moon Goddess. Even better, narrow it more to say: Diana the Protectoress. An example of an appropriate icon would be a silver bow and shaped like a crescent moon.

- The more you know and understand the Great One that you would Aspect, the more likely it is that you will succeed. If the Great One you are planning on Aspecting is a Goddess or a God, some research will usually unearth an assortment of names and epithets. Find the right one for the purpose at hand. The process of selecting or creating an icon is part of the preparation— don't skimp. Depending upon your tastes and visualization skills, the icon can be as simple as a geometric logo or as embellished as a heraldic device. Do not forget that the Great One has its own taste and sensibilities. Before making your final choices on the name and *the icon, place yourself in an open meditative state and see how the Great One reveals themselves to you. Ideally, this should be done days before the Aspecting. Even if a Great One is well known to you, do the preparatory work each time.*

V. Opening The Portal

A. Become aware of your Transpersonal Chakra. Some call it the personal Kether. It floats a few inches above the top of the head, and is normally centered over the place of the fontanelle. The fontanelle is the soft spot on the top of an infant's head that is also the location of the Crown Chakra. Activate the Transpersonal chakra by raising your hands and pointing skyward. Pull some energy down into your hands, then lower them to the place above your head that is the location of the Transpersonal Chakra. and pour energy out of your hands to create a ball of white light above your head. When the ball is stable, lower your hands. The Transpersonal chakra is the threshold between the microcosm and the macrocosm. It is the staging area from which Aspecting proceeds. If you find it difficult to open your Transpersonal chakra try the following: Imagine a line of brilliant white (or multi-colored energy) rising from the ground up through all your chakras. It opens into a fountain of light at the top of your head. You may wish to intone the "Eeee" sound as the light gushes from your Crown Chakra. Imagine the Transpersonal chakra as a sphere supported by the fountain of light.

B. Move your center of consciousness up into the sphere of brilliance that is centered on your Transpersonal Chakra. The more of you that rises, the greater proportion of each subtle body, the better. To facilitate this, try to rise up only through your central column of energy. Earlier in the Aspecting you constructed a pattern of symbols for the Parts of Self and an icon for the Great One. If you know that you have a tendency to become ungrounded or unfocused in ritual, leave these symbols and the icon where you created them. Move only your center of consciousness. This will help to keep you clearer. If on the other hand you have difficulty with letting go of control, move the symbols and the icon up into the Transpersonal Chakra at the same time that you rise up into it. This will help to lower your resistance to the experience. If you are working with a Great One whose nature is not a good match for yours or is foreign to you in some way, keep its icon down in the core of your center and create a second one in the Transpersonal Chakra.

C. Make sure that the place where you stand in the sphere of brilliance feels solid, stable, and centered. The brilliance may vibrate or softly undulate but it keep it as still as possible. Remember that you do have the right and the power to shape your surroundings in the sphere of brilliance. Many an Aspecting has faltered because the person has sunk down out of the Transpersonal Chakra and into their body. If your psychology demands it, create a surface to stand upon, one possibility is a white marble floor. Imagine it and it is so. Then say, (silently or aloud) "I Am Great' One's Name".

D. Proceed now with the work to be done in Aspect.

- *If you find that you are losing the Aspect before the work is done, visualize the icon that represents the Deity and repeat their name once more. If you fall out of Aspect completely, quickly return to the Transpersonal Chakra and visualize the icon. Don't restart the process from the beginning as this will draw you further out of Aspect and may disrupt whatever work is being done.*

VI. Returning

A. Return the focus of your awareness to being present in the sphere of brilliance. Look upon the icon you created as a point of connection to the Great One and see it fade away. If you left the icon at your center or had created two, dismiss the energy of the icon in the next part of this step. Re-affirm your name and thank the Great One that you have Aspected, and bid them part in love and peace.

B. Take a deep cleansing breath, and then descend down through your central column to where this work began. Make sure that all of you that rose into the Transpersonal Chakra has returned. Close down your psychic centers in whatever manner is your custom then ground and center. Whenever possible, it is good to touch the ground as your last action to release any residual energy.

- *It is very important that your focus of consciousness and awareness is fixed in the Transpersonal Chakra when you begin the process of ending the Aspecting. If you do not do this, there will not be a clean separation from the Great One and the creation of imbalances in your subtle bodies is almost a certainty. If the sense of presence returns shortly after the Aspecting has concluded, check to make sure that the icon is no longer in your energy field. Occasionally, a person will inadvertently recreate the icon by thinking too strongly on what they have just experienced. Sometimes this is brought on by other people asking them questions after the ritual. It is best to refrain from those sort of conversations until after taking some food and drink and a bit of time has passed*

Closing Thoughts

This chapter was written with a focus on the uses of divine embodiment within the context of ritual or in the service of others. Beyond those purposes, divine embodiment is a very powerful tool for personal growth and the refinement of the self. Within each of us there are many buds of undeveloped potential that only need the right conditions to unfurl. The intimate presence of a Great One within a person's aura, often offers the stimulus needed for these potentials to blossom. The blending of consciousness also offers new vistas and perspectives on what is already evolving within a person. One of the greatest gifts that can come from working with divine embodiment is that it is possible to gain capacities and insights that were outside your reach. Lastly, but very importantly, divine embodiment is also a devotional practice and is in fact a deep form of prayer and meditation. If a person wishes to open or to deepen their bonds to specific Great Ones, there is no surer route.

Spiritual Lineage, Egregores, & Sponsors

If a system of magick, a tradition, a religion, or a path is doing exceptionally good work, in all probability it was either created under the auspices of spiritual inspiration or was adopted by guiding presences after having proven itself as worthy. There are a myriad of ways in which the spirits support the work of magick on the earth plane and these are distinctly different than other forms of spirit contact. Although elaborated upon and refined by the work of living human beings, all the lore that is taught had its origins in the other realms. When a system of magick is worked in a consistent and coherent manner by many people for a long period of time, it becomes possible for the spirits to have a real hand in the shaping of the progress of that system. The spirits form a relationship to the evolving pattern that is that *system* separate from any contacts that they may have with individuals. The combined work of the humans and spiritual influences invests the system itself with energy, information, and essence; this is the *spirit* of the system. Contact with the spirit of a line or tradition is quite different from the other forms of spirit contact and tends to have a more shaping or formative impact on people. That does not mean that important and valuable work only occurs within established traditions. Some things are best achieved by individuals, some things are best accomplished by traditions that bear the marks of lineage, and it should be remembered that all systems and traditions began as small efforts.

Many of the ideas presented in the chapter "Ghosts & Ancestors" are prerequisites to fully understanding the material presented here. If you are in the habit of reading the chapters of books out of order or it has been enough time since you read "Ghosts & Ancestors" that memory has faded, please give it a quick scan before continuing.

Metaphorical Bloodlines

Spiritual lineage can mean many things to many people, often simultaneously. On the level closest to the mundane, it is like a family tree showing the history of the transmission of particular teachings. Like a genealogy it can show us how particular traits are passed from generation to generation or how certain things came to join the family line. In most formal magickal systems, the family tree branches most commonly through initiations or their equivalent. Spiritual or magickal lineage also means the passing of teachings, beliefs, techniques, and the ethos of the tradition. On an esoteric level it means a connection to the energy, information, and essence of the tradition in a manner that resembles that of a connection to the Ancestors of a people. On a psychological or social level, the sense of history and continuity can help to comfort and support people as they struggle on their path towards enlightenment.

It has been my experience that a significant number of people in modern esoteric communities scoff at the whole concept of lineage. In part I think that this is due to the scarcity of people with legitimate lineages, the large number of fakes, and a sad truth about every family tree. Having a lineage is neither a guarantee of talent nor wisdom, but it does make a difference. If you were looking to buy a racehorse, you would certainly inquire about its bloodlines, but the proof is in the performance. Spiritual lineage can also be likened to inherited wealth. Some will wear a rich heritage lightly and with honor while others will feel burdened, and some will confuse status with worth. Some will use their spiritual wealth for good, and others will squander it or grow miserly. Another reason why some people who are not affiliated with an established tradition may be skeptical of the concept of lineage is an unspoken implication that what they are doing is somehow less valid. This *implication* is a poison that needs to be drawn out of the collective consciousness of esoteric communities. All sincere spiritual work is valid so long as we serve our concept of the Divine in the manner that we are called to do so. Some serve best in traditions, some on solitary paths, and others serve best in the creative tumult from which new traditions arise.

Forms Of Transmission And Contact

Viable esoteric traditions are the keepers and the conduits for the wellspring that arises from collective spiritual work and collective contacts with spirits. The methods and practices used to maintain and to distribute this resource vary widely between traditions. Within themselves, traditions often make distinctions regarding the levels and types of access that its members have to this resource as well. It should also be remembered that traditions are indeed like a family tree, or more precisely like an actual tree.

Spiritual Lineage, Egregores, & Sponsors

Traditions are living organisms that are born, grow, reach their full height, decline, and die. Over the course of their lifetimes they also experience cycles that are internally and externally generated. What is transmitted is to some extent shaped by the tradition's place within its life cycle. A tradition in the season of its flowering will have an essence that is stronger with the force of creativity. A tradition at the time of its fruiting may have a greater flow of wisdom. As is true of the cycle of the year, there is beauty and purpose in each. Even close to the death of a tradition, it is possible to nip off a green cutting that may take root elsewhere. Consider these perspectives as you read the following paragraphs.

Direct Transfusion

In ancient times and in places today that keep to the old ways, each village or sept of a tribe would have someone akin to a shaman, a wise woman, a sage, a priest/ess. This person would seek out those that were appropriate for training to ensure the continuity of the teachings of the line. Because of the uncertainties of life, especially in a small population, there was a great pressure to make sure that there was always someone ready to receive the torch of the community's light and might. One or two unexpected deaths or life-changing events could be as perilous to the tribe as a hive losing its queen. In this setting the tree of tradition is really more of a vine than a tree.

There is more to making an apprentice than teaching them the lore, songs, chants, stories, history, and the magick. The making of an apprentice, who is ultimately an understudy and finally a replacement, also means infusing them with the energetic pattern of that tradition. Although it can be called many things, in essence it is an initiation, a beginning that cannot be reversed. This is similar to the grafting of a keying pattern to connect with the Ancestors, but it is more. The Ancestors can advise, motivate, and assist but they do not directly cause individuals to change. This infusion of energy, information, and essence acts as a catalyst that begins to transform the individual, to nudge them along the path of development that has been carved out by that tradition. If there are magickal and/or spiritual duties and responsibilities that come with this new status, such as healing or ritual work, this connection provides them with access to resources to do more than they could muster on their own.

Although rites of passage, or dedication, or acknowledgment such as baptisms, bar and bat mitzvahs, wiccanings, confirmations, the Asatru act of professing, etc. do create a linkage to the wellspring of a tradition, they do not force the issue of growth. Rather these gentle connections are like the addition of leavening to dough so that it may rise in accordance to itself. Those that are called, chosen, or begged into serving in a system of magick, a tradition, or a religion that has a living lineage, do not generally have the luxury of doing things at their pace. This is because the health and the effectiveness of the tradition in accomplishing its goals are blended with the individual's preferences and desires. There is an even greater weighting towards the common good if the individual takes on the role of what constitutes being a teacher or a clergy person within that tradition.

I said earlier that spiritual lineage can be likened to wealth, and it is so with each active member adding to this collective treasure house. When a great teacher, a great magician, a holy person dies it is a loss, but they can leave behind more than is immediately apparent. There are many stories of individuals taking a quantum leap forward upon the death of their mentor and sometimes this comes from a spiritual legacy. When a person dies, they shed their lower subtle bodies and these subtle bodies store much of the incorporate magick of that individual. These subtle bodies can be left as an inheritance to appropriate people of the same line. This poses no loss or danger to the person who has died; because, like their physical possessions, these are things they no longer need. It is risky for the person receiving this legacy. This process is more like a transplant than a transfusion or infusion. They must adapt and integrate these shells into their own subtle bodies in order to gain the gifts contained within them. They must absorb and subsume the totality of these shells. Depending upon the skill and intent of the giver, in addition to the desired magick there may be portions of the donor's personality, memories, desires, and frailties to be dealt with. This can cause the equivalent of an allergic or an immune response on an energetic level. Unless this can be resolved, there is the potential for harm to both the recipient and to the legacy. In the worst case scenario, the person is lessened by the attempt and gifts needed by their community are lost. When all goes well, the person is magnified and a spiritual resource is preserved. It should be self-evident that this course of action brings about a complex intertwining of personal and group karmas.

The higher the level of the spiritual evolution of the donor the more likely it is that the gift will have been purified and prepared to make it easier to take in. However no amount of skill nor effort will be sufficient if the candidate is unsuitable or unready. Occasionally, the spiritual legacy is greater in magnitude than what could be successfully managed by any of the available candidates, and sometimes the communal good is better served by dividing the legacy. This partitioning can only be done by a high order adept as it must be performed after death, which is not an easy task in the midst of such a transition. This practice is more common in the Eastern traditions, but it has been done in the West as well.

It should be noted that however the spiritual legacy is prepared or delivered, it is done so at some cost to what would have been integrated into the Ancestors. This is only a concern if the line in question has Ancestors which is often not the case with magickal orders. Even in tribal or ethnic groupings that do have Ancestors, often there is a separate energetic pattern that belongs to the overtly magickal members of that community. Another outcome from the giving of this type of spiritual legacy is that the spirit of the giver will be out of the reach of mediumistic talent for some length of time. The mechanics of the giving creates the consequence of a more complete disconnection from the flow of linear time earlier in the process of dying than is the norm. The trail is cold and cannot be followed and the spirit has not established its new address.

Egregores

An egregore (also spelled egrigor) is a thought-form that is created by a group of people through their collective will, imagination, and emotion. This can be a conscious or an unconscious act. All of us are connected to a large number of egregores because we are a part of many identifiable groupings of people. An egregore can be a very simple and relatively weak influence on the people from which it sprang or it can be highly sophisticated and quite powerful in its impact. Egregores also interact with each other in ways that can amplify or diminish their effects in those areas where their territories overlap. Most egregores, even very consequential ones, do not display signs of intelligence such as the capacity to adapt quickly or interactively. When this term is used in the context of the egregore of a tradition or a lineage, there *is* a guiding intelligence. Unlike most egregores, the egregore of a magickal organization is formed out of the highly focused states of consciousness generated by ritual, meditation, and other spiritual practices. Whenever a group does work to vision who they are as a group or what work they should be doing, this feeds the egregore guiding principles. When individuals who are members of a tradition do solo work that resonates to the pattern of their tradition, they also contribute to the egregore. Beyond this, some groups actively work to invest their egregore with additional strength. These types of egregores act as the gatekeepers and guardians of their tradition.

To understand the egregores of magickal traditions it is necessary to introduce a related topic, the magickal persona. The majority of systems stemming from the Western Magickal Tradition encourage their practitioners to create a magickal persona, also known as the magickal personality, as a part of their training and ritual work. This created identity is like a mask or a special garment that assists in modifying and shifting a person into the state of consciousness that facilitates magic. Over time the magickal personality can also be strengthened so that it can take on tasks. For example, it can act as an auto pilot that takes on the guidance of the magick when a person's consciousness wavers during a long or difficult working. The magickal persona can also be projected outwards to act as a second self in a complicated ritual or in one that requires the energy of the opposite gender when you work alone. The fetch, double, or co-walker are comparable concepts that for the most part fit within an extended definition of the magickal persona. Although the body of light overlaps with the magickal personality it is not one and the same. Whether or not the magickal persona is a help or a hindrance is primarily a function of how well it is integrated into the whole of the person. This integration must be an ongoing endeavor that can never be set aside as being completed. So how does all this relate to egregores? All the effort invested into the creation and the refinement of the magickal personality is exactly the sort of work that strengthens and evolves the egregore of that person's line. In fact, it is a valuable perspective to think of the egregore of a well developed tradition as being the analogue of the magickal personality but on a larger scale.

A highly developed egregore can also be thought of as acting like an incredibly powerful computer with expert system software. This can be quite impressive as when IBM's Deep Blue supercomputer beat Chess Grandmaster Garry Kasparov in 1997. Nonetheless, these systems, like egregores, are not self aware nor can they adapt past the boundaries of the models and the paradigms that they were given. In some respects, they are like lower level angels, devas, or elementals in that they are very good at what they do and very bad at what they don't do.

There are traditions that are actively opposed to the influence that egregores can have upon their members, including the egregore of the tradition. Generally this occurs in groups that value individual striving above all other considerations. In that context, egregores are seen as interfering, meddling, or restraining individual accomplishment and development. The formation of egregores is unavoidable as it is one of the natural outcomes of collective work, but it is possible to limit their impact. Some groups do this through periodic rituals designed to deconstruct the egregore. Other groups teach their members to become more aware of the impact of egregores in their life so that they may choose to ignore or resist their sway. Interestingly enough, by adopting a tenet that says that egregores are harmful, such a tradition creates an egregore that focuses on rooting out egregores other than itself.

Group Mind

There is something beyond the egregore, and that is the group mind. Many people use the term group mind as almost a synonym for egregore, but for the purposes of these discussions they will be considered as separate. Like an egregore, a group mind is constructed from the collective will, imagination, and emotion of a group, but it surpasses the egregore in that it is self-aware. At some point in its development, an egregore can achieve the level of complexity and flexibility that allows the seed of sentience to take hold within the thought-form. The source for this seed can be human in origin or it can come from whatever spirits are on the same path as that tradition. To return to the computer simile, a group mind is more like an artificial intelligence. It is prudent to treat the group mind of a tradition with all the due considerations that would be offered to a senior member of the line.

It is possible to have an actual dialogue with a group mind. It should also be said that *mind* does not mean a lack of emotions, drives, or motivations, this is a fully fledged consciousness. A group mind is both a child and a parent of the tradition that it serves. The behavior, character, and nature of the group mind arises from those that have contributed to its existence. It can be a very powerful thing and therein lies its virtue and its hazard relative to the healthy development of a tradition. Members of a tradition that have a strong bond to the group mind will have their capabilities augmented when it is invoked. Furthermore, those rituals and practices that belong to the tradition will invoke the presence of the group mind whether or not this is done explicitly. The group mind should be thought of as a spirit with all that suggests. Whatever nonphysical resources a tradition creates or fosters, such as astral temples and the like, are under the stewardship of the group mind. If an established tradition or line dies out, the group mind continues to persist for decades (perhaps longer) if not longer by subsisting upon the reservoir of accumulated energy. If that tradition still has significant unfinished work to be done in the world, the group mind will endeavor to re-create a body of members to fulfill its mission. I believe that one possible example of this phenomena is the reemergence of the Hermetic Order of the Golden Dawn.

Group Soul

One of the concerns that I have heard voiced about egregores and group minds is that they are soul-less and hence have the potential or tendency to do things that an ensouled being would not. I cannot follow this train of thought for very long before it derails. There is ample evidence of beings with souls committing monstrous acts and equally plentiful evidence of humankind being assisted by soulless entities. The fairy folk, elementals, and most of the nature spirits do not have souls, but we don't necessarily hold that against them. What is commonly called the soul is a particular part of the self whose primary task is to be the fluid within the vessel of evolution that we call incarnation. An individualized spirit produces a soul out of its own substance by sending a part of itself into denser planes of being. That portion of self that was sent forth is transformed as it conforms itself to the strictures of its new environments. The soul correlates to water, and like water it takes on the shape of its lifetime and dissolves into itself all the experiences. The soul is bound to the flow of linear time while also being linked to the spirit that hovers outside the frame of time. Does incarnation necessarily mean a body of flesh and bone? Not necessarily , but there must be a direct linkage to the physical plane in order to remain synchronized with the flow of time.

It is rare, but if the group mind of a tradition is sufficiently evolved and it is serving purposes greater than human plans, it is possible for the group mind to become ensouled. A spirit may choose to pour itself into the vessel that is composed of intricately composed thought-forms instead of one fashioned from flesh. By so doing, it ensouls the group mind. A spirit capable of such a feat is generally not human. It is possible for humans that have ascended above the need to incarnate to ensoul a group mind, but they are usually called to other tasks. An even rarer possibility, is the generation of a new soul out of the mingling of the soul stuff of the members. The equivalent of procreation can occur in the planes closest to the earth plane. A group soul does require that its *body* (the group mind) be firmly anchored to and nourished by the earth plane. There must be sufficient active, living, members to maintain the ensoulment.

A group soul contains within itself the energy, information, and essence of its tradition. It also incorporates into itself the egregore and the group mind in a configuration reminiscent of the reptilian and mammal brains forming the foundations for our higher functions. Under the guidance of a group soul, a tradition can reach heights that would otherwise be outside of its perception, let alone its reach. The overall thrust towards evolution is strengthened for all those connected to the group soul. This is because it has its own capacity for evolution, rather than having its development solely driven by the summation of the groups efforts. The synergy and polarity between the individual souls and the group's soul adds additional vitality and opportunities for exploration.

A group soul can experience the full range of emotions experienced by those that are incarnate. The most important of these is love. There are many forms of love, but a group soul has the capacity to love in a manner that humans can readily understand. It cares about its members and can express wisdom and instruction in a loving way. It is my belief that some of the Goddesses and Gods began their *lives* as group souls.

Contacts & Sponsors

All esoteric traditions, schools, and lineages have frequent contact with a variety of spiritual entities. This in and of itself does not constitute a contact. There are very few groups that experience any level of contact. There are more groups that claim contact than is the case. For some the assertion of a contact may be an honest error based on a lack of knowledge of the nature of contacts, and for others it is a calculated ploy. When a tradition attracts the interest and commitment on the part of one or more beings to form an ongoing relationship it can be the beginning of a new phase of the tradition's existence. For simplicity's sake, I will refer to the contact in the singular, but do remember that it can be plural. Please note that it is the being that makes itself known to the tradition, not the other way around. To intentionally seek a contact is almost always an invitation for disaster. There are many beings who might respond to such an invitation and not all of them are wholesome. When and if contact does occur, it may progress to the point of being a full sponsorship, with consistent Inner Plane contacts or it may forever remain a low level intermittent contact. There is no set model nor are there probable scenarios to describe this form of spirit contact and how it unfolds. Each situation is unique and the outcome hangs on the free will choices and actions of both humans and spiritual beings.

Mind Touches

The first contacts that a tradition or lineage usually receives are in the form of gentle mind touches. Key individuals within the group will have ideas, concepts, and inspirations dropped into their awareness through light, quick, touches to their minds. They may or may not be aware of the source for these ideas as the mode of transmission is normally clairsentient. With clairvoyance, clairaudience or the other *clairs* that express through a sensory modality, the individual generally knows that they are receiving information. A mind touch can be so subtle that when it rises from the preconscious into the conscious it seems no more foreign than one's own thoughts rising from the depths. Only individuals who have learned to trace the origins of their thoughts can reliably detect these gentle touches. At this point, the group may or may not be aware that they are being contacted.

Once the spirit has determined that the group will accept and will benefit from contact, the number and strength of mind touches increases. This change in the quality of the touches will often reveal to the group that they are being contacted if they had not become aware of it before. There are also palpable changes in the egregore or the group mind. If a tradition is to be contacted, it almost always occurs before the development of a group soul. For it to have the most benefit, contact generally takes place in the formative years of a tradition.

The mind touches differ from channeling or mediumship in that they do not require a trance, a focused receptive state, or any specific state of consciousness to be perceived. Moreover, they are initiated by the spirit, not the human. The stronger mind touches resemble true telepathy. After a time, the egregore or group mind becomes engaged in facilitating these contacts. This facilitation then makes it possible for members whose psychic abilities are below the threshold needed for direct contact to receive mind touches as well. Those individuals that are intrinsically pivotal or are situationally pivotal to the unfolding and implementation of the tradition's mission will receive the most contacts.

Overshadowing

For most traditions, mind touches are enough support and guidance for the work that they have before them. However, there are times and places where the threads of many possible futures converge or separate. and at those critical junctures something more may be required. In those circumstances a high order spirit make take a direct action. No doubt there are countless reasons that we cannot imagine which would prompt a spirit to do such a thing. Perhaps it sees that the probabilities are too skewed in a treacherous direction. Perhaps it is following the directive of a Great One and does what it does on faith. Or perhaps it sees an individual that has reached the verge of a great outpouring of creative work and chooses to be their muse.

Regardless of the cause or motive, the greater form of overshadowing resembles a sort of assumption of god forms except that it is set up from above rather than from within. The greater form is always a one to one relationship between an individual and a spirit. There is a lesser form of overshadowing that can be applied to groups of people that I will touch upon shortly. In the greater form of overshadowing, the spirit creates within itself a charged image of the person. Through the agency of resonance and affinity, this image becomes the instrument of communication between the spirit and the individual. The caliber of the communication hinges mostly upon the degree to which the individual has unified their various parts of self. Humans who have achieved consistent and clear communication with their higher selves will benefit the most from an overshadowing. The spirit endeavors to contact the person at the highest plane of being where the person's selves can remain conjoined long enough for conversation. The further along in their spiritual evolution an individual has progressed, the higher the plane of being where they can maintain lucid and unified consciousness. The higher the plane of being, the closer to the native plane of the spirit and hence the fewer distortions in the communication. The duration for this type of overshadowing can be as brief as a few weeks or can persist for decades.

Whenever a person who is being overshadowed quiets their mind and opens the linkages between their various parts of self, communication can occur. Embedded within the process of overshadowing there is a delicate yet profound form of communication. As in the assumption of god forms, the spiritual presence hovers over and surrounds the individual's consciousness. This spirit's presence *colors* the energetic atmosphere through which the individual sees the world. Although it is not the same as seeing through the spirit's eyes; over time as the person's inner eye adjusts, they will see a larger and more detailed world. Even if there were no other mode of contact in overshadowing, the change in perception and perspective alone would be enough to uplift the individual.

Groups of people can also be overshadowed. I refer to this as the lesser form of overshadowing because the quality of the communication is much lower and the duration is brief by comparison. It is more likely that the lesser form of overshadowing will occur where a member of a Tradition or an Order is already experiencing the greater form of overshadowing, but this is not a requirement.

The Astral Plane is not only the place where our thoughts can become forms, but also the terrain from which forms can become our thoughts. It is also a place where the location of things is based in large part upon meaning rather than physicality. People that are connected by an egregore, a group mind, or by ancestry can be thought of as existing in the same locus on the astral. There is an old maxim that states that the thought of one plane is the matter of the plane below it. The thought of a high order spirit easily shapes the terrain of the astral and in so doing predisposes those that are in that location to move in certain ways. Imagine a field of tall grasses, if a path is cut through the field most people will choose to walk the path. If you are in the depths of a forest, your eyes will be drawn to the place where a shaft of sunlight cuts through the canopy. There is no imposition on your free will in this form of spirit contact in that you may choose to walk where you will or think what you will, but only if you choose to be aware. It is also possible for a individual to experience the lesser form of overshadowing if the circumstances warrant such an effort. This differs from the greater form in that the spirit has not invested the time and energy to create a form to act as the instrument of communication. A mind touch begins the process to ready the individual. Then the spirit shapes the contours of the astral above that individual just as it would for a group contact.

Indwelling

This is an exceedingly powerful form of spirit contact that is so rare that in all likelihood you will not witness it directly though its affects shape the course of magick in the world. At any given time there are no more than one to three dozen individuals on the planet who are experiencing an indwelling. I had considered leaving this section out of this book but reconsidered it in the second draft. We live in the churning change of the tide from one Age to the next, and during such times the work done through indwelling is often especially significant. When a school, tradition, or line is said to be *fully contacted*, it means that one of its key members has taken an indweller. This is the closest and truest connection to a sponsoring being that can be made. This form of spirit contact has grave risks associated with it, but also the potential for work that can benefit many people over a broad expanse of time. Indwelling can best be described as a variety of divine embodiment that usually lasts until the death of the host. It is a great sacrifice on the part of both the spirit and the human because of the transformations and the obligations required of both parties. The successes and failures that come from this sort of partnership are scribed deeply into the fabric of things so the karmic consequences are greater as well. An indwelling only exists where there are critical nodes from which many potential futures can emerge.

There are very few candidates for taking an indweller because most of the prerequisites must be inborn and cannot be developed. The person must have an extremely fluid yet resilient psyche. They must be able to bend, shift, or blend as needed around foreign, often exotic, modes of consciousness and yet retain their own internal order and structure parallel to that of the being that they are hosting. Their ego must be developed enough not to disintegrate under the pressure of a greater consciousness and yet be pliant enough to commit to a life of service. The loss of true solitude is also more than many can bear, though it also is a blessing. The candidate must also have considerable active and receptive psychic abilities. Their subtle bodies and chakras must have the capacity to hold and to shape much more energy than is needed for the human form if the indwelling is to take.

Each indwelling is unique and different because it is the union of two beings. The spirit may be an ascended human or may be a being from any of the many different orders and streams of evolution. Sometimes these tutelary spirits are associated with the Goddesses, Gods, Demi-divine beings, or other Great Ones that are known in the stories told by humans. Sometimes they have no name or connection to that which we know in the lore. Some are best described by their elemental qualities or by their particular archetypal themes. Some are harder for a human form to bear than others. Depending upon the way that the human's and the spirit's energetic patterns interact, the human's life span may be lengthened or shortened. Not all indwellings take and this becomes apparent within the first several months and the spirit departs. It is possible to recover from a failed attempt, but there are always scars. When an indwelling is successful, it generally lasts for the duration of the human's life span. If the spirit must depart before the natural death of the person, it tends to bring on the death of the person. There are also similar though lesser impacts on the physiology and psychology of those that have a deep overshadowing.

It is possible to mistake a very profound overshadowing with an indwelling but there are significant differences. Those that have sufficient *sight* can see that the person's subtle bodies and chakras have been altered, and that there is a second consciousness within them. Unlike an overshadowing, the human and the spirit are never truly apart. A portion of one is always with the other albeit in varying quantities and with varying levels of awareness. In an overshadowing the spirit is communicating through resonance rather than through blending. An indwelling spirit may also borrow the body of its human host in a form of divine possession that allows them to act fully within the frame of time. The quantity of power that can flow from the spirit in an overshadowing is considerably less.

Indwelling allows a spirit to see and understand the world through human eyes which enables them to give guidance in a form that is better suited to the exigencies of the world. For the human partner, it opens vistas that it would take the journeys of many lifetimes to attain. Together it is a partnership that has the potential to great good as it bridges over the differences in energy, information, and essence that are artifacts of the structure of the planes of being.

Dangers

There are risks inherent in all forms of spirit contact, and there are specific dangers involved in contacts on behalf of a group. In all matters of magick and esoteric spirituality it is imperative that there be a balance between the forces that would overly inflate or deflate an individual's sense of self. Although all spirit contact can leverage this balance, adding the demands, desires, and interactions that come from being part of a group make this task more weighty. Those that have the greatest contact must strive against their own expectations and judgments as well as those that are collective. It is as grave an error to fully dismiss these feelings as it is to lend them too much consideration. One of factors that complicates achieving a proper balance is a misunderstanding of what it means for a group or an individual to be receiving support and/or contact. Too often people focus on the honor of the contact or the suggestion that it denotes a special standing relative to other people and groups. While this is partially true, it is healthier to focus on the greater truth which is that the contact means acceptance into training and service. The individuals and the groups under a spirit's tutelage are its students and its charges. Acceptance is not the same as performance. A student may be admitted to the finest university in their country and have access to some of the best professors available and still do poorly with the opportunity that they have been given.

Another sobering perspective comes from applying the simple adage, "work with what you've been given" to this circumstance. When a spirit has a task before it, it must contend with the limits of the earth plane and with human free will. It may be that another tradition or another individual would have been more worthy or more talented, but they chose not to participate. It may be that a group or an individual is selected because they are the only ones in a given geography and a given span of time that marks the the juncture of opportunity sought by the spirit. Even if the spirit is contacting the ones identified are their first choice, the group or individuals may have been slow in their development, and are called into service because the hour is at hand, ready or not. It is an honor to be selected and to serve, but be humbled in knowing that it is partly a matter of choice and partly a matter of making do.

Aside from the dangers associated with ego and human psychological frailty, there are hazards associated with the power of the spirits. The higher the order of the spirit and/or the level of the contact, the more likely that the contact will be mismatched relative to the capacity of an individual or of a tradition. This is especially true in forced choices based on the pressing needs of circumstances. To paraphrase Dion Fortune, a small boat with an overly large motor is unstable and hard to maneuver. Another perhaps less pleasant image is that of a small set of speakers connected to a high power stereo system. The speakers will begin to distort with the volume turned up to a quarter of the capacity and blow out at the half-way mark.

Closing Thoughts

Like the force of history, there are many currents that represent streams of spiritual evolution. The ultimate destination for rivers and streams is the great ocean which is the source of the waters, but rivers are not named for their destination. Spiritual evolution is about the journey and rivers take their names and their character from the land that they traverse. A spirit that acts as a sponsor, a patron, and a teacher is like the rain that causes the flood that cuts a new path for the river. It can be the earthquake that creates the waterfall or brings down the hills so that two rivers become one. A spirit can be the vein of gold that opens into a river so that its nuggets may be distributed. The possibilities are complex and manifold.

Traditions, groups, and lineages are also like a flock of geese in flight. One of the geese is the tip of the arrow that parts the air and bears the greatest burden. Those nearest the tip work nearly as hard as they continue pushing the winds aside. Those that are in that forward arrow see what is ahead first and must navigate. When the lead flyer tires, one of the nearer geese takes their place. Over time several different geese will take their turn at the tip of the flock. Most of the geese never work at the leading edge of the migration, but they all arrive. It should also be remembered that there are many flocks and many destinations even though the overall route is similar. Tutelary spirits can be thought of as the internal guidance the provides the timing and the direction for the migrations.

The form and the nature of spirit contact in lineages, groups, and traditions varies in accordance with what is needed. The power of a contact can wax and wane. When it is either no longer necessary for a higher purpose, or when a group diverges from its path or purpose, the contact is withdrawn. When a group has completed its mission it may lay fallow for a time, like a field resting before being furrowed for growth again. The force of life and evolution never rests, but the forms must rest at their proper period.

The Great Ones

There are limits to what can be known of the Great Ones, those beings whose evolution exceeds our own by so far that they are often called Goddesses or Gods, sometimes Archangels or the like. My personal belief is that ultimately the universe is a unity and therefore at the transcendent levels the Divine is one as well. Consequently everything is infused with divinity, life, and consciousness of various types and proportions. While we remain human, let alone incarnate, we cannot achieve contact with that most transcendent plane. We can only encounter the Great Ones that exist in the planes that our awareness is able to reach. The Divine is the universe and follows its laws, though many of them are unknown to us. The parts of the Divine that express themselves within the manifest universe individuate and become more and more specific and differentiated the closer they come to the Earth plane. This is how the many Great Ones can also be One. It is said that humans are a small reflection of the whole. The wheel of life, death, rebirth and evolution that humans undergo is a comparable reflection of the larger process of unfolding and development that is the life cycle of the Great Ones. Together the polarity, the current, of immanence and transcendence turn all these cycles from the smallest to the largest.

Some may feel that positing that we cannot commune with the ultimate face of the Divine is disheartening, I do not. A child in preschool is best taught by those whose mission in life is the education of young children. A chair from a university could have a go at teaching in kindergarten but the children would not learn any faster and it would be a loss to the older students that are prepared to receive a higher level of education. I am content to be in the presence of those *lesser* God/dess/es whose briefest thought contains more than all the thoughts I will have in this lifetime. If I ask you to imagine ten points of light, most of you will be able to imagine ten, but if I ask you to imagine ten thousand you will not be able to do so in anything other than an illusory way. Although the Great Ones that we can work with are less than the Infinite, they are functionally infinite for minds such as ours. Moreover, I am thankful not to be exposed to a greater light than I could bear. While it is true that growth often means going beyond your current limits, if you go too far past those limits there is destruction rather than development. We have known that the Earth and all its inhabitants are a small speck in a vast universe for quite some time. Science continues push back the frontiers of our knowledge showing us that relative to the whole we are smaller and smaller. The marvel and the mystery in all of this is just how big we are in our smallness.

Clothed In Dreams

The Great Ones do not have physicality or form as we know it, yet our contacts with the Great Ones often give us an impression of their characteristics. The same is true of many lower spirit contacts as well. In order to see the invisible, our consciousness clothes the unseeable with imagery, symbols, and sensations that we can comprehend. In the case of contacts with lesser spirits, the robe that we drape over the unseen is highly individual and idiosyncratic as it is mostly made from our personal storehouse of images. In general, the older, larger, or higher the spirit, the more of its *appearance* will be made from the collective impressions that have accumulated over the time that humans have worked with that spirit. All our thoughts and emotions create a trace, an impression on the planes above the physical. Most often these are fleeting impressions, but some can endure. One of the core teachings in the Western Magickal Tradition is that thought on a higher plane is the matter of the plane below it. This is a highly condensed statement and as such leaves out many nuances and can only be fully understood as a part of a larger body of knowledge, but it is the key to understanding how humans create the forms, the robes, that are worn by the Great Ones. If you simply reverse the statement, then the matter of our plane of residence becomes thought on the planes above. Our thoughts and our consciousness are a different *matter* altogether.

As has been stated before, through our subtle bodies we exist on many planes of being simultaneously although we generally do not have this awareness. In many spiritual practices people speak of raising their consciousness or raising their vibration. It is perhaps more accurate to say that they are connecting their awareness of their normal waking consciousness with higher levels of their own consciousness. When our consciousness is acting in unison or in synchrony on multiple levels, then we can create impressions, thoughtforms, on the other planes that endure and have consequence. This is one of the modes through which magick works. Only a small proportion of the population engages in magick, but the vast majority of the human race does engage in religious and spiritual practices. When people focus their consciousness on spiritual and religious pursuits, they raise their consciousness and unify their awareness. All the majestic temples, paintings, statues, poetry, and music that are the cultural manifestation of religiosity are but dim shadows of what has been created on the other planes through human devotion. Through the immeasurable efforts of countless souls over the centuries, richly detailed and elaborated thoughtforms have been created in honor of the Great Ones. These are the Deity Forms that are the robes that the Great One's don so that we might better commune with them. Just as a good teacher adjusts their vocabulary and the level of their discourse to students that they are instructing, so do the Great Ones select interfaces that we can understand.

There are a few points that must be clarified before continuing. It has been my experience that many people confuse or equate the Archetypes with the Deity Forms. The Archetypes are a small thing compared to the Deity Forms and are but one of the many components that fit within them.

The Archetypes are fashioned by the collective unconscious of the human race. The Deity Forms are created with the work and the input of all levels of human consciousness. More importantly, Deity Forms are made by the collaboration of the Great Ones with humans. These metaphorical robes for the Great Ones, we call Deity Forms, are tailored to fit individual facets of the Divine, they are not made whole cloth out of human imaginings. Over time, Great Ones make themselves known to the faith community that is their charge and suggest those changes that result in a Form that better fits them. We clothe them with our dreams which are a melding of influences. This is one of the reasons that Gods and Goddesses that have a long history will usually have highly developed and articulated Deity Forms. This refinement in turn facilitates contact with them and improves the quality and the lucidity of those contacts. Working with an established Deity Form increases the probability of contacting the desired entity because it resonates to them. As I have often joked in my classes that it is unlikely that Athena would choose to wear one of Aphrodite's robes, and Kali would have a pointed word or two with you if you tried to get her into it.

The Levels Of Deity Forms

This is my working model for the portion of the great chain of being as it applies to the various categories of entities that this book addresses. Having read this far, you should know enough about how I think and what I believe to have the context for this model. Please spend some time looking

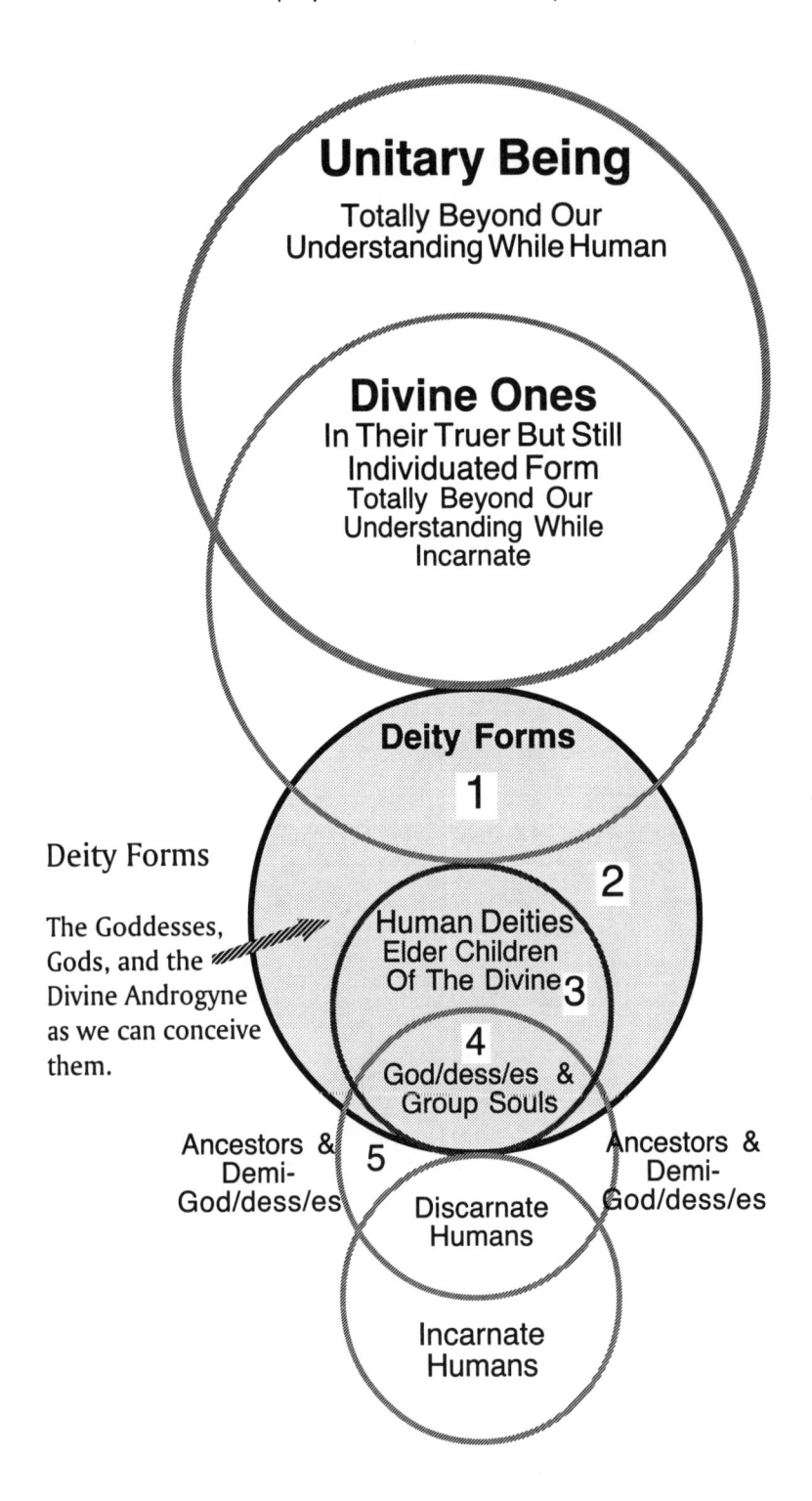

Unitary Being
Totally Beyond Our Understanding While Human

Divine Ones
In Their Truer But Still Individuated Form Totally Beyond Our Understanding While Incarnate

Deity Forms

1

2

Human Deities
Elder Children Of The Divine

3

4

God/dess/es & Group Souls

Deity Forms

The Goddesses, Gods, and the Divine Androgyne as we can conceive them.

Ancestors & Demi-God/dess/es

5

Discarnate Humans

Ancestors & Demi-God/dess/es

Incarnate Humans

The Great Ones

at the diagram on page 126 and thinking about it before reading its associated paragraphs.

The numbers in the diagram indicate the general classes of Deity Forms that are within the domain of the work of magick, religion, and spirituality. This diagram should be envisioned as three-dimensional, though in truth more dimensions are involved than can be easily depicted on a flat page. The top of the diagram represents the most ethereal plane and the bottom represents the densest plane. The gray sphere shows the level that contains entities that are generally perceived and labeled Deities. The areas of overlap and mutual inclusion should be interpreted as a accommodation to the fact that each category contains gradations of change from one to the other.

The Accessible Levels Of Deity Forms

I am presenting these categories of Deity Forms in the order of rising from lower forms to higher forms. For those that are on a metaphysical path, understanding comes from following the lines of connection in both the descending and ascending orders.

5 As this is the lowest level, there is the greatest degree of differentiation and variety in the Forms encountered. Often these are closely linked to specific and often local legends. Village, Tribal, and Ancestral Patrons, Deities, Heroes & Heras, etc. are here. Those that are called the Ancestors of the Mighty Dead in some traditions reside at this level. Those individuals whose greatness led them to becoming Ancestors can sometimes progress further and become the seed for a Form at the level of the Demi-God/dess/es. In syncretic fashion, some of these Demi-Divine beings can be correlated to each other and to Forms that lie above them.

The Forms of the Ancestors and the Demi-Divine Ones are enclosed entirely within the Plane of Being termed the Astral. In the terms of ethereal geography, they are the closest to us. This means that although time is not completely linear there, it has not changed so radically as to make correlations to our time difficult. Moreover the energy and subtle matter of the Astral can affect the Physical Plane with relative ease. These conditions explain how lower level Great Ones can still have a significant impact on the Earth Plane.

4 These are the Forms that are associated with the myth cycles of clearly delineated cultural traditions. They span a greater geography and have a longer history. Through the aggregation of the energy, information, and essence contributed by the prayers and devotion of larger populations over generations, they become highly developed, complex Forms. These range from individuated beings or group souls that function as Demi-God/dess/es to entities that are fully God/dess/es in their own right. These Great Ones contain all the previous lower Forms that were summed together as the pantheons of tribes were joined in the creation of the pantheons of nations. As you rise on the Planes there is a corollary process of unification of Forms based in thematic and essential similarity. In a manner of speaking, the smaller Deity Forms are like the past lives and/or Lower Selves of the larger Deity Forms above them.

This is also the level at which the Forms are available that can act as the emissaries and messengers from Great Ones on the Higher levels. They can be Messenger or Liminal such as Hermes and Hecate, or they can be beings that are identified as ArchAngels or their equivalent. Many of the Deity Forms who are in the role of psychopomp, guides to the soul in initiation or in death, also function from this level. In part this is because they resonate to the human pattern of the Three Selves quite strongly. These Deity Forms have the equivalent of a Lower Self in that lesser Deity Forms that were subsumed into them. They function out of a Middle Self that is the center of their awareness, and they are guided by the Deity Forms above them that are comparable to the Higher Self.

3 These God/dess/es are the future of the human spirit taken to its pinnacle. One of the ways that I conceptualize these beings is to think of them as the Elder Children of the Divine Source. If we think of spiritual evolution as occurring in waves like generations of cosmic proportions then these beings can be likened to our grandparents or great-grandparents. If the cultures that feed and maintain these Forms wither and fade, so do the Forms eventually. Do not confuse the Form that is merely an interface with the Divine Being that wears it. When power is poured back into an old Form, or new peoples create a fresh one in a classic style, it is filled once more by a Divine Presence. Just as some great human souls, like that of the Dalai Lama, continue their work from life to life in new bodies, so do some Great Ones in new Forms. Sometimes Deity Forms are reborn in cultures far distant in time and geography from their origins. Like an incarnation, the outer appearances will be different but the essence will speak its truth. That which is eternal inserts and asserts itself wherever and whenever its work is needed. The Great Ones that wear these Forms are few indeed.

Although these Forms and their associated God/dess/es at this level are far more than the Archetypes, it is at the this level the Archetypes reach their highest exaltation. These are the highest level of Deity Forms that derive their existence primarily from human efforts. This is not to say that the attributes and aspects of these Forms are not inspired and guided by Divine Beings, but rather that they are the expression of the highest aspirations of the combined levels of human consciousness of a people. These Forms speak to the depths and the heights of humanity. As a group these Deity Forms are the stars that mark the shape of the constellation that is the Human Oversoul; they are all our potentialities actualized.

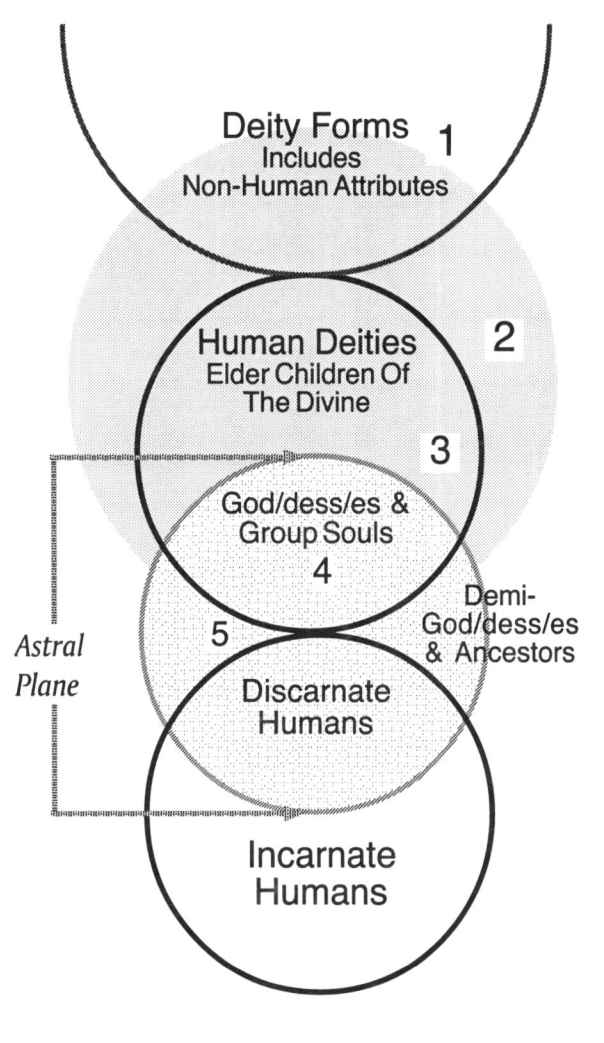

At this level and above it there is a great reconciliation of differences, the spirit of syncretism is strong. Here, all the Forms of the lunar goddesses are but the many garments in the wardrobe of *the* Moon Goddess.

2   These are Trans-Human God/Dess/es that encompass more than humanity. These we share with the other living beings of the Earth and the Forces of Nature. The term Trans-Human God/Dess/es is one that I just coined to

Deity Forms
1. Integrates Non-Human Attributes
2. Human Deities — Elder Children Of The Divine
3. God/dess/es & Group Souls
4. Discarnate Humans

Trans-Human Deities

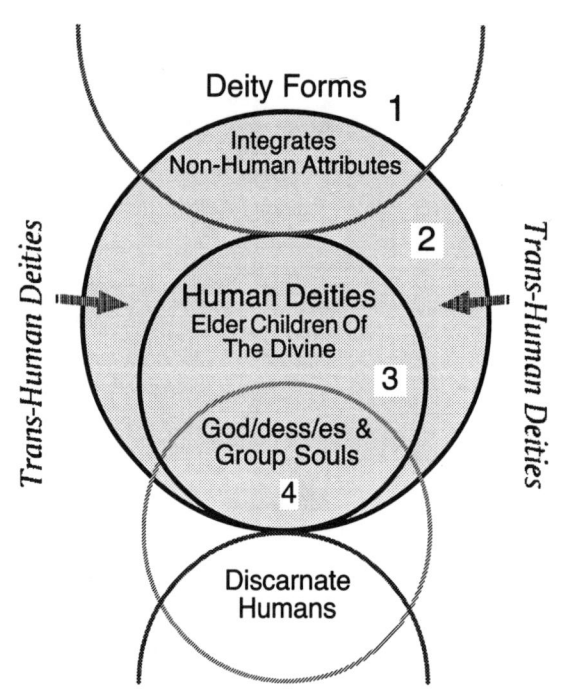

try to describe the nature of these Deity Forms. If you look at the areas indicated by the arrows you will see that these Forms span a range of levels from the lowest that I've described to above the level of the Human Deity Forms.

If we shed the nearsightedness of a human centric perspective, it is immediately evident that we are not the only living conscious beings on planet Earth. The life-force of the plants, the animals, and in (my belief system) the mineral and elemental beings also create Forms analogous to our Deity Forms but that are suited to their developmental needs and agendas.

There are Great Ones whose work and whose essence gives them a greater purview that requires a Form that is a mixture of human and nonhuman. Many of these are the God/dess/es that are represented as part animal or part plant. While it is true that humans have always looked to Nature for ideas, metaphors, and as an extended vocabulary to try to express the ineffable, it is in my opinion arrogant to presume that those Deity Forms that have hybrid attributes are solely a human creation. The Deity Form of a Goddess like Bast was built as much by feline souls as it was by human souls. As we rise on the Planes of Being, there are fewer boundaries and many of the human boundaries are merely provincial notions, not laws. Here we find Great Ones that can express themselves within a multileveled range of Forms that pertain to them. The goat-footed satyr can be an avatar of Pan, but Pan is also the Great God Pan whose name is all the life of the Earth, and all the steps between.

There are also Great Ones associated with specific elements such as Fire, Water, etc. Some of these fall into this Trans-Human category and some do not. In some of the Deity Forms that have elemental qualities, the elements

The Great Ones

are the elements as categories for human Parts of Self and as such are not Trans-Human. A Great One that has sway over the Elements is not necessarily of that Element any more than a human who has learned to work with the Elements is an Elemental. Those Great Ones that are truly of the Elements or of the forces of Nature are often marked by what appears to human eyes as identities with priorities and motives that are distant from human ones.

The highest of these Deity Forms are the vehicles for those Great Ones that are the stewards and the pedagogues for all the beings of this small corner of the universe that we call the Solar System. These are the Great Ones who choose to stay and do the work though they have integrated into one vision all the myriad perspectives of the younger spirits of Earth. They are the higher reflection of those human adepts who no longer need to be reborn but choose to remain connected to the Earth out of compassion. These are the Great Ones whose love completely exceeds our understanding.

1 These are the Forms that partake of all that is of Earth but are the dwellings of Beings of a broader Universe. They are closer to the ultimate nature of the Divine but still many levels removed from that ultimate unity. These Great Ones are rarely touched upon by incarnate humans in any manner except in speculations or imaginings. Up to this level, all the Deity Forms are the product of the life of Earth and the local influences of the Solar System. We live in a much vaster Universe. At this level, the Deity Forms are also shaped and informed by the contribution of other spheres of evolution, other waves of life, from beyond the locality of the Sun's neighborhood. All the God/dess/es that we work with, in all their majesty, are still small, though brilliant, facets in a Greatness surpassing anything we will be able to comprehend for countless Ages.

It is a very rare juncture in the flow of events that requires the direct intervention of the God/dess/es that function at this level. There is a summation of all influences, all energy, information, and essence as we rise on the Planes. This averaging of things tends to smooth out the rough edges, the noise, and inconsistencies of the lower Planes. Causality gives way to synchronicity as more points of meaning are plotted and the particles of moments give way to waves of reality. If some node in time and space is of such consequence that it remains evident and salient at this level, then it is a significant turning point that merits the attention of these Great Ones. In addition to taking a direct hand in these important junctures, these who are the highest of our Great Ones can and do work through the Deity Forms that lie beneath them.

Great Ones Embodying Great Ones

Think back on the various techniques described in the chapter "Divine Embodiment"; the principle of the small reflecting the large applies here as well. A Deity Form at a lower Plane of Being may act as an anchoring point, as a vessel, for a portion of a Great One from a higher Plane of Being. It is also possible for a Great One at a lower level to *embody* a Great One from a higher level. Consciousness on one level is the matter of the level below it. In some circumstances this embodiment occurs between beings that are unique and distinct from each other. In other cases, it is the equivalent of the Higher Self of a human connecting more fully with the Middle and Lower Selves. This is especially true for God/dess/es that whose Forms and history show them to operate at multiple levels or scales of grandeur.

When there are particular moments in time where the disposition of the future balances on a point and can fall in many directions, these linkages of embodiment between Great Ones can extend down to the level of divine embodiment in humans. If a human is engaged in divine embodiment and the need at hand exceeds the capacity of the Deity Form that has been called and the need merits attention, the Great One that they are embodying can reach upwards. Depending upon what is called for, this chain of linkages can reach from the Earth Plane to the highest levels we can conceptualize. This is one of the means by which a major Divine Presence can intervene deeply into linear time and dense matter. It is not within our power to bring together such a set of linkages. This only occurs when our higher will and a Greater Will make a common cause of acting in the here and now.

Blessings That Full Fill

I have observed that it is fairly common for people to have expectations and desires that are higher than are needed in their daily lives. This is also true in the practice of magick, religion, and spirituality. When we invite the participation of the Great Ones in our lives and in our rites, they appear to us. How they manifest is their choice, not ours. Do not assume that if you call upon an elevated aspect of a Great One, that they will come in that

The Great Ones

Form. Be open to perceiving what is present, not what was desired, and your understanding will deepen. One of the marks of human wisdom is seen in knowing how much is enough in any given occasion. Grace in action is an elegant balance of neither too little nor too much. As any ritualist worth their salt knows, excess power that is not shaped, contained, or directed can lead to woe or worse. It is in the wisdom of the Great Ones to offer blessings that fulfill, blessings that full fill. They send enough to fill our need to the brim and no more, but even here we still make our own choices. Humans being human, it is still possible for us to tilt, shake, or drop the chalice and spill what has been offered. Moreover, if we offer a cracked vessel it can leak or shatter with the pressure of its contents.

Let me give an example of expecting a visitation commensurate with the purposes at hand. Putting modesty somewhat aside, I make very good vegetarian food and I have fed many people at spiritual events in our home over the years. Let us say that for some unexpected reason, the Dalai Lama had some reason to travel to the rural corner of Sussex county where I live. I could certainly extend the invitation for him to come and break bread with the locals, but I would not expect him to come. At best, I would receive a pleasant thank you note. If, my spiritual community had a standing relationship of good service to the local monks, then perhaps the invitation might merit the Dalai Lama sending an emissary on his behalf. The only reason that I can imagine that the Dalai Lama himself would come is if his guidance indicated to him that this small and humble event would lead to some greater good. When we invite an important personage to our homes we don't presume that they will come, only that they will respond appropriately. The same holds true for the Great Ones.

Whether or not you, metaphorically speaking, come face to face with a Great One while you are incarnate does not prevent you from receiving their blessings to the degree that you are able. Just as our lives can be touched and changed by the words and deeds of admirable people who lead by example, so can we be touched and changed by whatever level of contact we experience with the Great Ones.

Of Spirits: The Book Of Rowan

"7th Sight"

Closing Thoughts

Truth comes in many modes and in many forms, and is often a matter of scale and perspective. It is a generally accepted truth today that we are all travelers on a world that is a ball flying through the heavens. Those privileged few humans who have traveled in space and have beheld all of the Earth in one glance know this to be true. Long before we could orbit the Earth, some came to believe this truth through the proof offered by science and others believed for reasons of the soul. In past generations, those seekers that stood on the summit of a mountain, or stood on the peak of a spiritual experience were afforded the opportunity to sense this truth. There are truths that are deduced by the powers of the mind and truths that are uncovered by the powers of the soul. The truth of *informed subjectivity* that is one of the foremost goals for those working with the spirits requires the powers of both the mind and the soul.

Those that work diligently with the spirits, are given opportunities to see truths comparable to the majesty of the blue-green gem of the Earth floating in the velvet of space. Unfortunately, not everyone rises to the challenge of such opportunities. Even if they do learn a truth from a being of greater wholeness, the vision does not always lead to experience and understanding. By definition, the universe is of one whole and encompasses all of creation. This simple truth should be the key to greater understanding, but often it is not enough. The simplicity and the magnitude of this truth can trick the mind; the mind balks at trying to imagine the size of the whole. The mind races outwards until it crashes against the limits of its power and imagination, and then often retreats to the small safe boundaries of the letter of the truth. The spirit of this truth is not fully lost because a portion of it is present within each letter, each bit of the truth, and every bounded place no matter how small it may be. A larger portion is gained when the scope of the mind rejoins with the Parts of Self that do not think in words. As the various subtle bodies, levels of Being, integrate and unify, the person's spirit contacts can be processed through a truly informed subjectivity. As the powers and the scope of the Self develops, the golden key of unity opens doors into larger and larger domains of truth.

Of Spirits: The Book Of Rowan

The mind may be the source of some of the challenges to spiritual work, but its refinement is essential to spiritual development. Many writers and teachers from esoteric paths put a considerable amount of time and effort into convincing students of the very real limitations of the mind/personality duo. Indeed, the brighter and the more promising the student, the greater the potential obstacle to their spiritual growth if they identify themselves primarily with their intellect. However, there are also very serious limits to spiritual evolution that is unbalanced by the lack of intellectual development. When there is commensurate development, the Higher Mind as well as the Higher Heart emerge as functions of the Greater Self. Without this union, spiritual communication and communion may very well lead to blind faith, confusion, and that strange form of idolatry that is called fundamentalism.

The Dream Of A Tree

Imagery is one of the tools that helps us to bridge the gaps between our various Selves. Pathworkings, also known as guided visualizations, take us on those journeys of no steps that lead us inwards. In the appendices of this book you will find a pathworking entitled "The Dream Of A Tree" that I wrote to assist in the process of discovering linkages between the many Levels of Being. There is some benefit in reading it but there is no substitute for listening to it as it was intended to be used. It is best if you can find a trusted companion to read you the pathworking. If you cannot, record a tape and listen to it. Do not listen to it more than once a month and it is advisable to keep a journal of your experiences.

The Book Of Ash

My next book will be Spirits of Earth And Faerie: The Book Of Ash. In it I will extend what has been offered here into an exploration of nature spirits, plant spirits, animal spirits, elementals, and the many beings that reside in Faerie. I will also offer my thoughts on the ecology of the Planes, how the various streams of life weave the broadest web.

Thanks & Blessings

I give you my thanks for accompanying me on this journey. I wish you the fullest blessing that you are able to receive.

Appendices

The Square Of Abeyance 138

The Ontogeny Sigil 139

The Tattva Symbols 140

The Dream Of A Tree Pathworking 141

The New Alexandrian
Library Project* 145

A Dream Whose Time Is Coming* 147

Poem: Coronation Day 148

About The Author 149

* These are projects that I strongly endorse. Please read them.

Of Spirits: Appendices

The Square Of Abeyance

Casting-
1. Draw a line of matte black energy from North to South. Then one from East to West. You are in the center.

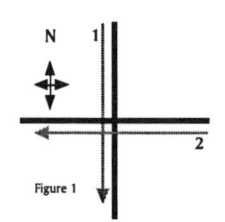

2. Create a square outlined in matte black. Starting in the N.E. fill each square in sequence with the gray energy of active neutrality*.

3. Examine the Square and make sure that every part is filled with gray energy.

4. Will away the matte black boundaries. The Square of Abeyance is complete.

Figure 1

Figure 2

Gray Energy: The gray energy of active neutrality is like the static of a radio or a television tuned to a missing station. It is like white or pink noise in that it contains many frequencies but in no particular pattern. It is neutral in its indecision rather than in being an average or in being indefinite.

Dismissal- The maker of the Square need only introduce into the Square a spark of energy of any bright color and the Square will fade away. With the Square of Abeyance it is possible for the maker to leave the Square after it is cast and dismiss it at a distance. This may be particularly useful if the Square was used as protection against unpleasant energies.

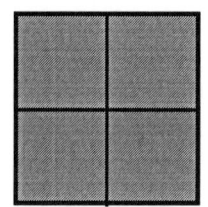

Figure 3

Description- The Square creates a space where energy patterns and frequencies that are not native to the physical plane of reality are made null and void. They are held in abeyance which depending upon their nature results in stasis, dismissal, or dissolution.

Figure 4

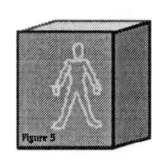

Caution:
Most people find being inside a Square of Abeyance feels oppressive because their psychic senses are often blocked by the Square. Many sensitives are head blind inside the Square. There is no lasting harm but it can be frightening.

Figure 5

More material on this method is found in *Castings: The Creation Of Sacred Space*.

Of Spirits: Appendices

The Ontogeny Sigil

The Ontogeny Sigil is part of a set of 49 symbols that have come to me through my work with the spirits and with the integration of some past-life memories. I first started to record the impressions that led to this sigil around 1983. You may take the origin of this sigil with a grain of salt, but my experience of its efficacy over the years proves its practical worth.

The Ontogeny Sigil and the other symbols in this set are multidimensional and are in constant motion when I see them with my mind's eye. Part of the work in making them useful for others has been in finding the proper way to flatten them into sigils that can be drawn. The sigil represented on this page works as a key to access the more complete version on the other Planes of Being.

The word ontogeny means the inception, the process, and the progression of an individual organism from embryo to adult. I named this the Ontogeny Sigil because it has the effect of encouraging a person's energetic pattern to return to its normal courses. My psychic perception of it in action is that it holds then reflects back only those energetic patterns that most closely align with the essence of an individual. It does not filter out foreign patterns, rather it stimulates the individual's subtle bodies to force out what is not their pattern.

The color of the energy used to charge and to activate this sigil should be blue-green. The exact shade can vary but try to go for a color somewhere around turquoise or aquamarine. This color is used because the energies that are associated with it are on the threshold between the organic/pranic energies and the raw elemental energies of nature. This blue-green vibration is often found in many of the interfaces and boundaries between the Planes as well.

To use the Ontogeny Sigil, make a copy of it that can be held. It may be a simple paper version or an elaborate wood carving or whatever else you like. In this case the material does not matter but fidelity to the geometry does. Ideally, the person should look at the sigil, but at the very least they should be touching it. Have the person sit in a comfortable position and give them the Ontogeny Sigil and ask them to look at its center. Scribe a circle around them using blue-green energy that encloses them and them alone. Stand outside the circle and chant: "Ahhh-Liiihh-Tawhnn" Let the "nn" sound hang in the air before each repetition. Continue chanting until they indicate that it is enough or you can see that it has helped. "Ahhh-Liiihh-Tawhnn" is the name of the place the spirits said that this sigil comes from. I have noted that this chant activates the Heart, Third Eye, and Solar Plexus Chakras in that order.

Of Spirits: Appendices

The Tattva Symbols

    These symbols and colors are a common variant of the Tattvas (Hindu in origin) that were popularized in the West by the Hermetic Order of the Golden Dawn and should be familiar to those with Ceremonial Magick background. For many Neo-Pagans the symbols to not make immediate poetic sense as icons for the Elements or Parts of Self. Likewise, the color scheme of the Tattvas does not match the color schemes commonly used by Neo-Pagans. Because of the concentrated and coherent work that has been done using these symbols and colors, they have strong thoughtforms that can be drawn upon. I strongly recommend their adoption as your primary associations for these concepts. I have found the Tattvas to be very useful and have intuited visual associations that ground them in the bardic sensibility of Neo-Paganism.

    Air is represented by a blue circle that depicts the blue dome of the sky, the air that surrounds us. Thought, like the blue sky, encompasses us, but is not the limit of the heavens.

    Fire is represented by a red triangle that is a stylized flame, sharp edged with the bite of fire. It points upwards as it is the soul guided by spirit.

    Water is represented by a silver crescent that reminds us that water's true color is the color of light, and is ruled by the Moon.

    Earth is represented by a yellow square, yellow for gold, the highest vibration of matter, and yellow for sulphur, matter in its lowest vibration. The rectilinear solidity of a square with the echo of the four quarters in its form.

    Spirit is represented by an egg that may be black, clear, or all colors that stands for the infinite possibilities of creation within the parameters of its order.

The Correlations To The Parts Of Self Are Not Traditional

MIND	SOUL	HEART	BODY	SPIRIT
Blue (circle)	Red (triangle)	Silver (crescent)	Yellow (square)	Clear/Black/All (egg)
Air	Fire	Water	Earth	Ether
Vayu	Tejas	Apas	Prithivi	Akasha

Of Spirits: Appendices

The Dream Of A Tree Pathworking

Close your eyes and move inwards. Take a deep breath and become aware of any distractions from the outside world— sounds, sensations, thoughts and feelings that came with you to this ritual. Gather these distractions together ••••• and bid them depart until you return from this journey. •••••

Open your eyes briefly and then close them again holding within yourself the image of where you are in the here and now. This will help you to return later

All that is, is a soft darkness in every direction and above and below. A velvety richness of black with shadowy suggestions of crimson and purple that you breathe in and breathe out with ease. ••

You float comfortably, upheld by the billowing of the velvety richness that fills your senses. • You feel a touch across your face as soft as the gentlest breeze, so soft it could have been just imagination. Then you feel it again. You feel a rhythm. You feel it pass over you like a ripple on a pond. A ripple that repeats again and again and again in the fabric of all that is. •••

The rhythm carries you... pulse by pulse... beat by beat .. ••• You move carried on the gentle pulsations. You begin to see a hazy, glow in the velvety distance. You can't make out the details of the form yet but it is growing larger and brighter. Closer and closer you come on waves made of the immaterial void. Your eyes can see enough to begin to make guesses at what they see. •••

You see a Tree so vast that the whorls on its bark are galaxies, its fruits are quasars, brighter than all else in manifestation. It's roots reach into depths beyond the reach of time and light. It's crowning canopy is the edge of the universe itself. Be in awe of its majesty ••• •••

You have moved near a root. It draws into a dark vortex that shifts and becomes a tunnel. You move faster and faster and faster. ••••

You burst into the center of the Tree. A place of color, sound, scent, vibration . A place of constant motion and utter stillness. ••••

You lose consciousness in the extremity of fullness. ••• •••

Of Spirits: Appendices

You are. You become. You become aware. You see that you are a Star Seed hanging upon the Universal Tree. • • • You sense the twinkling light of the million myriad of other Star Seeds. • • • •

A great Wind shakes the Tree. You and swirls of other Star Seeds are cast forth from the Tree by this wind.... You see a nebula below you. The ripples in the glowing gas are like the furrows on the cortex of the universal Mind. The furrows are the gentle soil that you fall into. • • •

From a seed you expand outwards, like a carefully folded wing stretching to its maximum reach. You are a Tree within the Great Tree. • • • •

See how each Star seed has grown, See yourself as a tree in the midst of the Great Forest. Your roots are reaching out and intertwining with the roots of all the other trees. You feel the essence of community in knowing that you arise and are nourished by the same soil. Communion and communication sparks from your roots to their roots like the crackling lightning of synapses. • • •

Your roots are delving down into the ground. Your roots are slipping through the soil, embracing the ever larger stones that they find as they dig deeper. Your roots continue intertwining with the roots of the other plants and trees that surround you. Your roots and the roots of all the trees that you sense around you are digging downwards towards the Earth's core. The Earth's core is a fiery ball of molten rock and your roots reach towards it. • • • • •

Feel the Fire of Evolution that rises from the core of the Earth. Feel it course into your roots, charging them with the mission of growth.

Now feel your boughs and branches reaching upwards to the sky. Feel the breezes move through the leaves that are your fingers. Breezes that carry the wavefronts, the vibrations, of everything word, song, and thought that has ever been or will be. • • •

As you reach upwards towards the blazing sphere of the Sun, feel the light touches of the leaves and the branches of other trees reaching skywards with you. Feel the warmth of the Sun upon your leaves, your branches, and your boughs. • • • • •

You are reaching higher and higher. Your boughs reach the Sun and hold it in a wide armed embrace. • • • • • Slender branches continue reaching higher towards the wispy flares of the Sun's corona. Your perceptions follow the branches and then the tips of the highest twigs. There, past the highest tip, a flare of light reaches down and touches you. • • • • •

A sound deeper than french horns, deeper than the rumble of the Earth turning, shakes the branches. • • •

You vibrate from root to tip, your trunk coursing with life. • • • • • Twig by twig, branch by branch, bough by bough, and down the trunk, the tree begins to glow as if lit from within.

Take time to glory in the feeling of the Sun above you and the fire of the Earth's core below. • • • •

You find the center of your consciousness, the point that is the seat of your awareness has become sharply focused. Let your center of consciousness float free, up and down in your trunk. Let your consciousness float until it finds a place of stillness and balance between the Sun above and the fire below. From that center place look at the Tree that you are • • • • • You are the Tree of your Lives. • • • • •

You hear a distant voice calling you with a sound that is your name though it is no name given in human tongues. • • •

Your consciousness descends down the trunk, following the call of your name that exists beyond names.

At the base of the tree lies a powerful serpent, its coils moving in a slow spiral. What does the serpent look like. • • • • •

Held carefully in its moving coils is a red egg. From glance to glance the egg changes as it moves in the coils, sometimes brilliant like a ruby other times a dull leathery red. • • •

Look now into the serpent's eyes and ask it if it has anything to say to you. Listen. • • • • •

Accept the silence or the statement and dwell on it. • • • • •

The serpent asks you to enter the red egg. Your center of consciousness leaves the tree and moves into the center of the red egg. Within the egg you see every possible shade of red, swirling about you. You see crimson, scarlet, tulip red, cherry red, rose, fire ember red, and many other shades you cannot name. • • • • • The swirling colors fade and you can see through the crystalline shell of the egg. • • • • •

You look up at the tree and see that it has become winter. The tree is bare. Snow is heavy upon the boughs and icicles weigh down the branches. The serpent lies in a still circle about the roots. Within the egg you feel warm and safe at the same time that you are aware of the cold wind that blows outside. • • • • • The snow and ice begins to melt. • • • • • Soon all traces of winter are gone and the buds begin to swell. Flowers blink open, covering the tree. The flowers' fragrance is faint but distinct.

The flowers fade and fall as leaves unfurl and turn from the light green of spring to the deep green of summer. New branches grow and twigs spread out to catch the intense warmth of the Sun.

Some of the flowers have set and have swollen. • • • • • The leaves have caught with the fire of autumn and are ablaze upon the branches. The wind that whistles outside the crystal egg has chilled. You notice a particular crimson fruit that hangs heavy upon the tree. It is egg shaped and translucent. The fruit is ripe. It falls and is caught in the coils of the serpent. • • • • •

The crystal egg that you are inside of begins to crack and to crumble. The outer shell vanishes and you are afloat in a red mist. The mist grows darker and you sense that you are in motion. • • • • • The motion stops. The mist clears, and you find that you are now at the center of the fruit that is now the new egg. The serpent turns its head towards the egg and bids that you depart. You leave the egg and become the tree once again. Your roots dig towards the fire of the Earth and your branches reach towards the Sun above.   • • •

The world ripples, changes, fades. You float comfortably, upheld by the billowing of the velvety richness that fills your senses

See the place where this journey began. • • You flutter your eyes open and find yourself back in the here and now. Back in the place where we began. Back in the place you held in memory so that you could return.

Take a deep breath. Move your toes and fingers.
Be here and in the now - Be here and in the now - Be here and in the now.

— *End* —

The New Alexandrian Library Project

This project is working to create a library worthy of its namesake. By no later than 2010 the New Alexandrian Library will open its doors.

A Modern Resource For Metaphysical Communities

The Vision

Have you yearned for a place where the sacred sciences are preserved and the future of esoteric knowledge is explored?

We live in a time where there is a new renaissance in the exploration of the spiritual and the magickal. A need exists for a place where knowledge from many esoteric traditions can be accessed by scholars and serious seekers. The New Alexandrian Library will be a modern, state of the art library with the capacity to preserve and to protect all forms of esoteric knowledge.

Books, periodicals, special collections, music, media, digital data, etc., will all be carefully cataloged and cross-referenced to ease the work of research. The Library will work to restore and to preserve rare and damaged documents. The history of our magickal communities will also be collected for the future. In addition to its physical presence, the New Alexandrian Library will have an internet component to maximize its utility. Over time, as much material as is possible, within the limits of logistics and legalities, will be available online.

The New Alexandrian Library will be primarily a research and reference library, not a lending library. It will provide onsite workstations and other facilities. We are also examining housing options for long term research.

The land for this project is being donated as well as the architectural plans. The New Alexandrian Library will be located in the sacred woods of Seelie court in Southern Delaware. The New Alexandrian Library will be under the aegis of the Assembly of the Sacred Wheel and as such donations are tax deductible.

The New Alexandrian Library Project

Would you like to leave a legacy that will be treasured by generation upon generation of seekers on the path?

Inclusive Of All Traditions

The New Alexandrian Library will be collecting materials from all spiritual traditions. Like the original Alexandrian Library in Egypt, it will be an interfaith crossroads.

Your Part

You can be a part of bringing this dream into reality. Although donations of books and other materials will be welcome, the immediate need is for the funds to build the library. There will be a sculpture of a tree in the library that will bear the names of those that make sponsoring donations. The names will be on small plaques in the shapes of leaves, flowers, fruits, and stars.

$250 - $999 —Leaf
$1000 - $2499 — Flower
$2500 - $4999 — Fruit
$5000 & Over — Star

Make your tax deductible checks payable to:
The New Alexandrian Library

Donations Of Any Size Are Welcome

The New Alexandrian Library Project
14914 Deer Forest Road
Georgetown, DE 19947
(302) 855-0699

NAL@sacredwheel.org
www.sacredwheel.org/nal.html

Will you help to open that door?

The New Alexandrian Library Project is sponsored by the Assembly of the Sacred Wheel a 501(c) 3 religious nonprofit organization

The New Alexandrian Library Project

A Dream Whose Time Is Coming

21 Chants
For Rituals And
Devotional Ceremonies

Art © Helena Anderson

Recorded under a full moon in a temple dome in the forest of Seelie Court. The sound is powerful, real, and filled with the magick of the moment of its creation.

This Audio CD
Is A Fundraiser For
The New Alexandrian
Library Project

To Order It Directly

Send $16 with $3.00 for shipping ($1.00 for the shipping of each additional cd) to:

The New Alexandrian Library Project
14914 Deer Forest Rd.,
Georgetown, DE 19947

Or ask your local music or metaphysical store to carry *A Dream Whose Time Is Coming*

For More Information:
www.sacredwheel.org/dream.html

1. Airy Messenger
2. Call To The Moons
3. Endless Eternal
4. Cernunnos
5. Epona
6. Feral Beauty
7. Earth Spirits
8. Herne Who Hears
9. Holy Well & Sacred Flame
10. Holy Earth Mother
11. Sun Return
12. Oh Visions
13. Great Mystery
14. Samhain Revels
15. Sweet Magick
16. Maiden Of Mysteries & Sunfire
17. Isis, Aset
18. Stars We Were
19. Waters Of Life
20. And The Wheel Turns
21. Thanks Turns The Wheel

Total Time 45:00

Coronation Day

On distant Alytan,
Long lost to the sight of the living
   Hidden not in time, but by the shrouds of memory
   Hidden not in time, but by the drunkenness of disbelief
   Hidden not in time, but by the film that gauzes desolate eyes

There... on distant Alytan
Deep within the living skies where the nights
   Are filled with the birth waters of stars
   Are filled with moons as numerous as stars
   Are filled with the lightning of Jovian worlds

There... when in the rolling dance of the Spheres,
The figure of the Bridge appears
Then it is Coronation Day on Alytan

In every field, in every valley
Through every street, through every path
On every white peaked mountain, on every white capped sea
The people prepare for the Moment

Voices rise in praisesong mingled
Instruments call an answer to the ringing sistrum
The ringing sistrum
Hung high, hung high on the Hill of the Tree
Each soul on distant Alytan
   Lifts hands to the heavens
   Lifts hands to the heavens

It is Coronation Day
Each Soul swears fealty
It is Coronation Day
   A crown of lights of hammered flame appears above each head
   A crown of lights, lucent with the fires of their Spirits
Appears high above the Hill, high above the Tree
It is Coronation Day
   Each Soul swears fealty to the crown— the crown of their divinity

In the Moment of the Bridge they remember
There on distant Alytan, long lost to the sight of the living,
They remember.

   By Ivo Dominguez, Jr.

About The Author

Ivo Dominguez, Jr. is a writer, an artist, a visionary, and a practitioner of a variety of esoteric disciplines. He has been active in Wicca and the Neo-Pagan community since 1978, and has been giving workshops since 1982 on Chakras, Divination, the Qabala, Ritual, Astrology, Herbalism, and other topics. He has taught at Sacred Space, Etheracon, the Free Spirit Gathering, Ecumenicon, The Crystal Ball, Stones Rising, and many other events. He is the convener for Between The Worlds, a conference that occurs once every few years when the astrology is right.

Ivo was a founding member, and a past High Priest, of Keepers of the Holly Chalice, the first coven of The Assembly of the Sacred Wheel a Wiccan Tradition. He now serves as an Elder to the four covens of the Assembly. His techniques are rooted in a synthesis of traditional metaphysical teachings, modern science, and memories from past lives. He has been published in numerous periodicals and is the author of *Castings: The Creation of Sacred Space* and *Beneath The Skins*.

He is one of the owners/stewards of Seelie Court which is 102 acres of wooded land in Southern Delaware. The land at Seelie Court is filled with magick and has been consecrated to the purpose of deepening all pagan paths. For more about Ivo go to: www.sapfire.com/ivo

Of Spirits: The Book Of Rowan

"Portal Of Earth"